IN SEARCH OF THE LIVING GOD

Roy Warke

In Search of the Living God

BIBLICAL REFLECTIONS

the columba press

First published in 2000 by
the columba press
55A Spruce Avenue, Stillorgan Industrial Park, Blackrock, Co Dublin

Cover by Bill Bolger
Cover photograph by Eileen Warke
Origination by The Columba Press
Printed in Ireland by ColourBooks Ltd, Dublin

ISBN 1 85607 296 7

Acknowledgements
The poem quoted on page 43 is from *A Diary of Private Prayer* by John
Baillie, Charles Scribner's Sons, New York, 1949, and is used by
permission of Simon and Schuster Trade Division.

Contents

Foreword

The great binding cord running through the bible is the activity of God. Notable figures come and go, nations rise and fall, situations are highlighted and fade, but through all the changing scenes the eye of faith discerns the hand of God.

What follows is an attempt to tease out the contemporary implications of God's activity in a variety of circumstances depicted in the bible. The thoughts expressed were first preached in a variety of settings throughout the Church of Ireland, in particular during sixteen years as Rector of Zion Parish, Dublin, and more recently as Bishop of Cork, Cloyne and Ross.

I soon discovered that the transposing of the spoken word to the written page is never easy, not least in terms of topical illustrations. However, there are certain core elements which must always form part of Christian exegesis, and my hope is that the essential baby has not been thrown out with the dated bathwater.

Some of the sermons have been reproduced virtually as delivered, while in other cases they have been curtailed and only some salient points have been transcribed. Either way the aim has been to highlight the activity of God in the affairs of people and nations.

I am indebted to my wife Eileen for typing and proofreading the manuscript, and to a variety of individuals, who, over the years, made helpful comments from the perspective of the pew.

Roy Warke
October 1999

CHAPTER 1

Genesis Chapter 1 Verse 1:
'In the beginning God ....'

This is the central statement in the bible, and significantly it occurs in the very first verse. It introduces the theme which runs through the bible from start to finish – God active.

In the Old Testament the emphasis is on God active in creation, history, nations and individuals. In the New Testament we learn first of God's activity in revealing himself through Jesus Christ, and then later through the Holy Spirit in the life of the church as that infant community grew and matured.

Despite the appearance of many famous characters in the bible, the real hero is always God. Moses and David and Peter and Paul only come to life because of their relationship with God. People followed them and were inspired by them because they were aware that God was with them. The Children of Israel promised their allegiance to Joshua on the threshold of the promised land only in so far as they could be assured that God was with him as he had been with Moses (Josh 1: 15-16). Again, the powerful preaching of Peter on the day of Pentecost (Acts 2) moved people because it was obvious that God was with him.

Despite the battering which the institutional church is taking at the present time, a battering often prompted by its own culpability, there is evidence that interest in matters spiritual is in no way diminished, rather it is to be found in less regimented forms characterised by such modern phenomena as informal house groups and visits to Taizé.

From a different slant and geared to the commercial world, Charles Handy, in his highly acclaimed book *The Empty Raincoat,* instances Vaclav Havel, the playwright turned president, who has argued 'that we will only avoid "mega-suicide" in our time if we rediscover a respect for something otherworldly, something beyond ourselves.'

Over twenty years ago one of the most powerful publishers

in England, when asked what he thought people wanted the church to tell them, replied that the church's business is to talk about God, because people want to know what God is like and what he is doing.

If we accept that there is this continuing interest in God we must go on to examine the nature of that interest.

Is it one of deep concern, or is it merely one of detachment? A detached interest in God may be no more meaningful than the passing interest we might take in the latest political story from Leinster House or the most recent revelation from Buckingham Palace. In other words, our interest may not be deep-rooted or personal, or involve us in any commitment. If that is so, then our interest in God is really peripheral, something that will vacillate with changing spiritual fashions.

However, there are many for whom the search is genuine, and who seek a renewed understanding of God's will. For such it is important that they are not confronted with a distortion of God, sometimes created out of an exaggeration of a genuine characteristic or through an attempt to mould him to our worldly ideals. Such distortions have resulted in frequent caricatures – a merciless judge, a vindictive father, a benevolent grandfather, a vague impersonal force, a remote supreme being or an upholder of the establishment.

Where then do we look for the image of the invisible God? Is it not to Jesus Christ? That is why we return over and over again to the gospels in our search for the knowledge of God. There, in Jesus Christ, we see God revealed to the fullest extent that we can understand. 'He who has seen me has seen the Father,' said Our Lord, and that is our guarantee of the nature of God, the God who was and is active.

CHAPTER 2

Genesis Chapter 4 Verse 7:
'Sin is crouching at your door'

The Hebrew word for 'crouching' in this very telling phrase is the same as that used in ancient language to describe an evil demon crouching at the door of a building to threaten the people inside. (The New Revised Standard Version speaks of 'lurking'.)

In a sense sin is always like that, crouching ready to pounce and latch on to whatever opportunities are provided in our lives.

The closing verse of Genesis 1 states: 'And God saw everything that he had made, and indeed, it was very good.' But sin soon entered in and humanity experienced the Fall. The result was what is technically described as 'original sin', which is outlined in the words of Article 9 of the Thirtynine Articles of Religion: 'Original sin standeth not in the following of Adam ... but is the fault and corruption of the nature of everyman, that naturally is engendered by the offspring of Adam; whereby man is very far gone from original righteousness and of his own nature inclined to evil ...'

This inclination to evil is graphically outlined in the familiar story of Cain and Abel. There we have described not only the first murder in the bible but also some of the other elements that so often go hand in hand with the fatal act. In this case there was jealousy, anger, deceit and lies, a real catalogue of the works of the flesh. They were all compounded in the person of Cain, illustrating just how far man had fallen from the original workmanship of God.

Today we are still prone to sin and we have only to look around us in the world to realise how often the tendency is translated into a specific act of evil, even murder.

When this happens, a variety of solutions are propounded. For some the answer is to counter force with force, and we don't have to look too far in time or space to see the futility of that course of action. For others it is to be found in integrated education in the belief that if people, especially young people, are educated together they will grow up appreciating each other's point of view. Still more seek an answer in appropriate political structures and the example of tolerance which public figures can give.

Few would deny the value of education or political action, but more and more it is being realised that what is required is a fundamental change of heart, a spiritual experience which counteracts the tendency to sin. In all the discussion following the paramilitary ceasefires in 1994 very little was said about the volume of prayer which had been offered up over the previous twenty-five years. William Temple once said that if we pray for courage we must not be surprised if God gives us opportunities to be courageous. So having prayed for peace, should we be surprised if God has answered us positively by turning the hearts of those involved? Here indeed is a real challenge to our faith.

To experience a change of heart does not mean that we may never do or say or think anything evil again, but it does mean that the thrust of our lives has been altered and the general direction is now signposted to God.

For some this is a dramatic and traumatic experience, symbolised by Paul's experience on the Damascus Road. For others it is more gradual, as with Timothy who from childhood had enjoyed the benefits of a religious upbringing. Whatever the experience, it involves the recognition of need, which is so often the case when life turns sour. Here the need is for the grace of God flowing from the Cross of Christ where the victory over sin was won. It has been expressed succinctly by one writer: 'Man needs not to be made better, but to be born anew – from above. The Cross is the remedy for sin.' (E.J. Bicknell: *A Theological Introduction to The Thirtynine Articles*)

However, two further points need to be made. The first is that this actual experience of change is taking place today, sometimes in the most unlikely circumstances. Even before the ceasefire of 1994, paramilitaries from both sides of the divide in Northern Ireland had experienced this change of heart and together were visiting schools to give witness to the fact of the grace of God.

The second point is that change can only be effective and progress maintained through effort. It is only as we work at the spiritual element in our lives through prayer, bible study and worship that enrichment will follow. There are no short cuts, no instant fixes. Supermarket-style spirituality is a transient commodity. It is one of the interesting facts of religion that the more deeply spiritual people are, the more conscious they are of sin crouching at the door and therefore of the need to work at their faith.

CHAPTER 3

Exodus Chapter 5 Verse 2:
'Pharaoh said, "who is the Lord, that I should obey him ...
I do not know the Lord".'

History is liberally dotted with journeys of epic proportion. In recent times men and women have sailed singlehanded round the Cape, Everest has been scaled and hitherto unknown regions of Antarctica have been charted.

In the now highly civilised continent of North America, few stories can be compared to the rigorous journey of the early Mormons from the East Coast to their present headquarters in Salt Lake City.

Yet dramatic though all these journeys have been, there are few that bore the same epic qualities as the exodus of the Children of Israel from Egypt some three thousand years ago. Anyone who has visited the Holy Land and seen the wilderness at first hand can but marvel at how they survived and had the will to keep going in such circumstances. For the Jewish people, it is the focal point in their history, and when Leon Uris sought a title for his novel telling of the birth of the modern State of Israel he looked no further than the one word he knew would stir the imagination of many people – *Exodus*. For the Christian, the Exodus is one of the most descriptive analogies used for deliverance from the bondage and slavery of sin. As ancient Israel was saved by God from bondage in Egypt, so the new Israel is freed by Christ from the bondage of sin.

Egypt at the time of the Exodus was ruled by the Pharaohs. The particular Pharaoh in power at the time of the Exodus was regarded as one of the greatest builders in Egyptian history. Excavations that have been carried out, not to mention the pyramids, testify to the ingenuity of those ancient craftsmen. This architectural genius, allied to the readymade workforce supplied by the Children of Israel, resulted in a powerful creative combination.

But many Egyptians also lived the good life at that time; a life of material plenty and leisure. Hunting, fishing and boating were the favourite pastimes of noblemen and their ladies. The picture is that of a self-satisified, materialistic society sowing the seeds of its own destruction.

In many ways there is a frightening contemporary ring about all this, even down to the words of Pharaoh – 'Who is the Lord that I should obey him ... I do not know the Lord.' And just as Pharaoh's reply to Moses was laced with contempt and smugness, so too the attitudes of many today bear the same characteristics.

Of course people are free to reflect this attitude. That is the nature of the freedom we have as human beings; a God-given freedom. But it is the contention of Christians, backed up by the experience of centuries, that the true end of humanity is 'to know God and enjoy him for ever', as is expressed in the Westminster Confession. Not just to know about God as a type of academic study, but to know God in the depths of one's being and one's experience. It is this knowledge, in the deepest sense of the word, that gives unity and purpose to life and supplies us with the values that make life worth living.

People come to this knowledge of God by many avenues. Some experience it through the wonder of nature – 'The heavens declare the glory of God and the firmament showeth his handiwork.' At a time when interest in Celtic spirituality is on the increase, this avenue of nature is being trodden by many feet.

Adversity is another avenue along which some have travelled, even severe sickness, and many a hospital chaplain can tell of lives transformed in the most unlikely circumstances.   The phrase 'creative suffering' is no empty shibboleth, nor should it be, for those whose faith is based on a crucified Saviour.

Nor must we discount the traditional services of the church, although these are often designed to nourish a knowledge already there. In terms of traditional services, the setting is often conducive to the development of faith, and many have found their knowledge of God immeasurably deepened by attendance at a Cathedral Choral Evensong.

Sometimes people come to a knowledge of God despite themselves. The flight of Francis Thompson is repeated in the hearts of many, while others can reflect the experience of C. S. Lewis, recorded in his autobiography, *Surprised by Joy:* 'The steady unrelenting approach of Him whom I so earnestly desired not to meet. That which I greatly feared had at last come upon me.'

However, the most oft trod avenue to a knowledge of God is the bible, read, marked, learned and inwardly digested. It is this fact which gives grounds for optimism at the present time when there is evidence of renewed interest in the Word of God, judging by reports from Bible Societies across the world.

And so the words of Pharaoh come echoing down the centuries: 'Who is the Lord that I should obey Him ... I do not know the Lord.' But God is active. He has spoken and is speaking in many ways to the hearts of men and women. When they hear his voice and respond to it, life takes on new meaning and fresh purpose.

CHAPTER 4

Exodus Chapter 33 Verse 16:
'What else will distinguish me and your people
from all the other people on the face of the earth?'

Moses was coming to the end of a long hard journey. He had led the Children of Israel out of slavery in Egypt. Shortly they were to enter the Promised Land of Canaan. In this land were many tribes, some of them fierce and warlike, without any knowledge of the one true God. For Moses it was a time of concern. The people had already murmured against God on their travels through the desert. Why, they asked, had God led them out from the comparative comfort of Egypt to die in the wilderness?

How then would they face up to and survive in these new and difficult conditions?

Moses knew they could only survive by being true to the principles and ideals that had ensured their survival in Egypt and on the hazardous journey in the desert, that was by putting their trust in the living and active God. 'What else,' he says, addressing the Lord God, 'will distinguish me and your people from all the other people on the face of the earth?'

The question posed by Moses, like so many questions in the bible, is timeless, but nevertheless it must be placed in the contemporary setting. And so we ask, what are some of the distinguishing marks of the Church of Ireland today?

The first and very obvious mark is that the Church of Ireland has a minority status in this island, and in some places it is a very small minority. In parts of North Cork it is no more that 1%. Historians may delve into the reasons for this disparity and even be critical of the circumstances surrounding this phenomenon, nonetheless it is a fact of life with which we must live.

Preaching on the occasion of the Consecration of George Otto Simms as Bishop of Cork, Cloyne and Ross in 1952, Eric Abbott, later to become Dean of Westminster, chose as his subject 'The Little Flock', based on words from Luke 12:32, 'Fear not, little

flock; for it is your Father's good pleasure to give you the kingdom.' In the course of his sermon Dean Abbott said, 'A minority
is always in a state of peculiar temptation; it swings between
pride and despair; it is prone to too much introspection ... But if
a minority is to avoid the temptation to be too self-concerned
and too self-regarding, it has to turn its eyes to the Cross of Jesus
Christ not only for consolation in its solitary faithfulness, but
also for strength in its outgoing power. Jesus Christ, the
Shepherd and Bishop of our souls, hung on that cross alone, but
its outgoing power into all the world is Almighty Love.' And he
concluded, 'We must be that kind of minority.'

On the cross we see the paradoxical intermingling of weakness and power, a minority of one from whom there flowed the
power of Almighty Love. To act as channels of that outgoing
love is the task laid upon every branch of the church and on each
individual member. For a minority, it poses a particular challenge when the natural pull is towards introspection.

Although a minority, albeit a minority with its roots deeply
embedded in the ecclesiastical soil of this land, the Church of
Ireland is very conscious that it is part of the totality of Christian
witness on this island and further afield.

Ecumenism, that often misunderstood (and mispronounced!)
expression, is no optional extra in the life of the church. It is at
the very heart of the divine. The unity of the Godhead must be
reflected in the unity of the church. As it has been expressed by a
leading Irish theologian, Seán Freyne, 'Even the Christian theol-
ogy that is three in one should remind us that a diverse unity is
not a compromise to weakness but rather an expression of the
full richness of life.' Our Lord's prayer 'that they all may be one'
must give urgency to the continuing search for unity, and the
building of bridges of reconciliation at all levels, ranging from
local to international, should be a priority for all churches. That
is why the concept of unity by stages contained in the report of
the first Anglican Roman Catholic International Commission is
so important. The principle is to build on whatever has already
been attained. To take one step at a time and not be disappointed

and frustrated if full organic unity at times appears a long way distant. One has only to look back over the last forty years to realise that there has been movement in this whole area of church life. For a minority, it is not an easy road to travel and many still fear absorption. But without in any sense forfeiting what has moulded a minority in terms of doctrine and practice, the promotion of ecumenism must be a distinguishing mark because it is the will of God for his people.

One way in which a minority protects itself from isolation is to see itself as part of a body greater than itself. For the Church of Ireland this is possible in two ways. In the first place it can see itself as part of the multi-church tradition in the country, with a contribution to make to the ongoing debate on many issues of vital importance. The Christian voice is not necessarily a unified voice on all issues and on occasions it needs a minority view to fill in the overall picture. The Christian tapestry on this island is a rich and varied one, gradually becoming more comprehensive, particularly as new liturgical expressions emerge.

In the second place, each national church is part of a world-wide fellowship and for the Church of Ireland this is the Anglican Communion, with some seventy million members in every continent, and growing rapidly in many places, especially in parts of Africa.

The question posed by Moses had within it both personal and communal elements – 'me and your people.' And we must never neglect the personal element. But the main thrust is communal. This is very clear from the comment of Moses: 'How will anyone know that you are pleased with me and with your people unless you go with us?' God with us, that is the distinguishing ingredient, and in the long run it must be the truly distinguishing mark of any church.

CHAPTER 5

Deuteronomy Chapter 34 Verse 1:
'Then Moses climbed Mount Nebo from the plains of Moab
to the top of Pisgah, across from Jericho.
There the Lord showed him the whole land ...'

One of the most dramatic speeches to have been captured by the
media in recent years and preserved for posterity on tape, is that
delivered by Martin Luther King on the night before his assassination in 1968. He was speaking on the eve of a civil rights rally in
Memphis, and it was almost as though he had a premonition of
his death. In that distinctive southern drawl, he spoke of the
progress that had been made in the Civil Rights campaign and
of what still remained to be accomplished before the black people of America could claim that they were indeed free and equal
citizens of that great country. With dramatic impact he drew
upon the Old Testament character of Moses to drive home his
point. Moses, who had led the Children of Israel out of slavery
and through the wilderness to the brink of the Promised Land,
which he had glimpsed from Mount Nebo but had not entered.

And so the speech moved forward to its climax as Martin
Luther King with deep emotion said: 'I have been to the moun-
tain top and I have looked over and I have seen the Promised
Land. I may not get there with you.'

We all have our vision of the Promised Land, our Shangri-La
or Utopia. Usually it is bound up with peace and justice and
freedom from want and suffering. For the Christian there is the
further dimension of unity with God through Jesus Christ. As
we are incorporated into him at baptism, and as we are nourished through worship and sacrament, so we come into closer
union with God, which is our ultimate goal. Using Paul's words,
'I press on towards the goal to win the prize for which God has
called me heavenwards in Christ Jesus' (Phil 3:14).

However, the Promised Land, if it is to be something more
than a general ideal, must be earthed in specific realities. There

is a time to deal in principles and a time to be specific, a time to plead for peace and justice on a broad basis, and a time to ask more direct questions. Certainly this was true of the ministry of Jesus. He gave his followers the general principles upon which to base their lives – 'My command is this: Love each other as I have loved you' (Jn 15:12). But he did not hesitate to give specific directions when the situation required it. To the tax collectors he said, 'Don't collect any more than you are required to' (Lk 3:13), and to the soldiers his response was, 'Don't extort money and don't accuse people falsely – be content with your pay' (Lk 3: 14).

What then are some of the specific elements we would like to see as part and parcel of our Promised Land? Such a list is bound to be arbitrary and coloured by personal preferences, perhaps even prejudices. Let me suggest two.

The first is truthfulness. One of the basic commandments is, 'You shall not give false testimony against your neighbour' (Ex 20:16). And yet at times how difficult it is to get at the truth. It becomes overlaid with interpretation until the original facts become distorted. One has only to read the four accounts of the gospel to realise how perceptions differ depending on circumstances.

Today there is the further complication of living in the age of the mass media where competitors vie with each other in their graphic headline presentations in order to attract readers. In such circumstances truth is often the first casualty in the search for 'a story'.

This leads on to the second element, which is honesty. There appears to be an attitude abroad today which views honesty as naïve, and what really matters is not being found out. Hence the necessity for tax amnesties, the pursuit of television licence dodgers, and beef tribunals. It is part of a national malaise in a country which is professedly Christian, but where the external trappings do not always signify an inner core of truth and honesty.

In relation to the Promised Land, it is tempting to dream the impossible dream. But is it unrealistic to think in terms of a land noted for the twin virtues of truth and honesty? Without them the heart of any nation beats very weakly indeed.

CHAPTER 6

Joshua Chapter 24 Verses 15 and 16:
'... choose for yourselves this day whom you will serve,
... Then the people answered,
"Far be it from us to forsake the Lord to serve other gods".'

The right leader is very important in any enterprise. The captain of a team can transform his players from a haphazard group of individuals into a well-drilled unit. The right manager of a firm can promote *esprit de corps* among the workers. The general of an army can mould the separate divisions into a co-ordinated striking force. 'Change generals,' said Sarsfield at the Battle of the Boyne, 'and we will fight you over again.'

History abounds with examples illustrating the importance of leadership in every walk of life, and nowhere is this more evident than in the bible, and not least in the Old Testament. One such leader was Joshua.

During the difficult journey of the Children of Israel from Egypt, Joshua had been captain of the army, with the unenviable task of protecting a straggling band of wanderers led by Moses. But within sight of the Promised Land Moses died, and Joshua took over full control.

His experience as a military leader was to serve him in good stead as the itinerant group faced a host of warlike tribes and were enticed to follow strange gods and indulge in heathen rites and practices. Like all good leaders, Joshua placed the issues clearly before his people and called for a decision, '... choose for yourselves this day whom you will serve.' Choice and decision were the factors involved on that important occasion.

All through life we are involved in decision-making. It is this which builds moral fibre into our character. The decisions we are called on to make may vary in substance and importance. They may be trivial, such as the colour of the new car or what cereal to choose for breakfast. Or they may be more serious such as what career to aim for or what person to marry.

For many, an important choice comes at Confirmation when a decision is made concerning the particular path of life. It is a responsible individual choice when, to quote the Confirmation preface, they 'publicly profess their faith in Christ'. It is not something done on the spur of the moment or on a wave of emotion, but is the culmination of a process involving school, Sunday School, parish and home, climaxed by a period of more intensive instruction.

At Confirmation we make a definite and deliberate decision to follow in the path of Jesus Christ. 'Do you turn to Christ?' It is no mere formality and should never be treated as such. Above all, it calls for perseverance because the Christian road is difficult, and never more so than today. The imagery of John Bunyan's *Pilgrim's Progress* highlights some of the difficulties as Pilgrim journeys to the celestial city. *The Slough of Despond* and *Hill Difficulty* are reflected in so much of the stress encountered in life today. *The Valley of Humiliation* is a symbol of the ridicule and scorn which many Christians face in society. *Vanity Fair* reminds us of the temptation to forsake service for superficial pleasure.

Just as the Children of Israel encountered difficulties on entering the Promised Land, warlike tribes, strange gods and heathen rites, so too we encounter our difficulties and our temptations. But to have made a definite decision, to have taken a cool and calculated step forward, is half the battle. It gives a foundation on which to build. This was what the Children of Israel found and so they could reply to Joshua, 'far be it from us to forsake the Lord to serve other gods.'

CHAPTER 7

Ruth Chapter 1 Verse 16:
'But Ruth said, "Entreat me not to leave you
or to return from following you; for where you go I will go".'

Loyalty is a characteristic much admired in a person. In the Book of Ruth we have a very good example of this virtue.

The story tells of Naomi, a Jewess, who with her husband and two sons moved from their homeland, Judah, in time of famine, and settled in a foreign country, the land of Moab. Her husband died, and her two sons, who had married, also died.

By this time news was coming through that the famine in Judah had passed. Naomi, like many another exile, longed for home, and so she set out to return with her two daughters-in-law, Ruth and Orpah. They were both natives of Moab, and Naomi, no doubt conscious of the problems that awaited them as strangers in a strange land, where national identity was of vital importance, urged them both to remain behind. If both had remained who would have blamed them? There was no real obligation on them to return, and the uncertainty of the way ahead was daunting.

Orpah did remain behind but Ruth returned with her mother-in-law to Judah. The way the bible puts it illustrates the depth of loyalty she displayed: 'Where you go I will go, and where you lodge I will lodge; your people shall be my people, and your God my God; where you die I will die, and there will I be buried' (Ruth 1:16-17). Later Ruth's loyalty was to be rewarded when she was taken as wife by Boaz, one of the richest men in the district.

It is tempting to look on the story of Ruth as an example of loyalty and nothing more. Indeed if it was nothing more it would still be a story well worth telling. But like so much of the bible, when we quarry a little deeper the book yields up even more riches. As Richard Holloway, in his book *Behold Your King*, says of the contemplative use of scripture, 'looked at steadily and pondered slowly it yields up new meaning and we know it for the first time.'

To begin with, the Book of Ruth was written some centuries after the events depicted in it. Although set in the time of the Judges, that is before the kings of Israel and Judah were established, it was written after the return of the Jews from exile in Babylon hundreds of years later. Indeed it has been described as an historical novel.

When the Children of Israel returned from exile, they were faced with a problem, the problem of living alongside pagan neighbours. What were they to do? How were they to relate to them? It is an age old problem. Two courses of action were open.

On the one hand, they could live in isolation as though the other people did not exist, maintaining their own traditions, culture and religion, and attempting, as the bible put it in another place, to keep themselves unspotted from the world. And this was the course of action strenuously advocated by some of their leaders, as the books of Ezra and Nehemiah bear out.

On the other hand, they could acknowledge that there were other people in the land and attempt to live with them as neighbours, even intermarrying. This is the course of action which the author of Ruth was trying to put across. The people were being urged to have faith and courage to step out from their ghetto-type existence and come to grips with reality, a reality which they might not much like, but which was nonetheless a part of their lives.

Translated into modern terms, it is the recurring problem of the relationship between church and community, and at heart this is what the Book of Ruth is all about. The Old Israel after the exile found itself in a new and difficult situation calling for a readjustment of attitude. So too the church, the New Israel, is in a difficult situation today.

One course of action is for the church to turn in upon itself, to busy itself with institutional and ecclesiastical concerns and forget about the community at large. This is a particular temptation for a minority church tradition. It is regarded as a safe course of

action typified by non-involvement and non-exposure. But it
has within it the seeds of self-destruction. When the then
Archbishop of Canterbury, Dr Michael Ramsey, once said at a
meeting of the World Council of Churches in New Delhi, 'the
church that lives to itself will die by itself' he was saying nothing
new, but merely underlining a basic fact of ecclesiastical life. Of
course some time must be spent on domestic affairs and to de-
cree otherwise would be folly. But it must not get out of proportion, as can easily happen.

The other course of action is for the church to reach out and
meet the community, becoming aware of and involved in its
problems. Indeed if the church does not take this course of action it is being untrue to its divine commission, 'Go ye into all
the world.' Nor is it responding to the divine initiative of the
Father who reached out to the world by sending his Son to be
our Redeemer. As it was once put, the church is not just the
redeemed community; since it is the Body of Christ it is also the
redeeming community.

If the church does not reach out to the community it results in
a loss of vision and stunted growth. In the eyes of the world it
means irrelevancy, which is often the accusation levelled by the
younger generation. It may be dismissed as youthful exuberance and typical of the modern age, but it should challenge the
church to heartsearching both as an institution and in terms of
individual membership.

But to reach out is the task of the whole church and not just
individual members, as has often been the case. It is all too easy
for the church to bask in the reflected glory of individuals of
vision – a Martin Luther King, a William Temple or a Pope John
XXIII, or in a more modern era, Desmond Tutu, Gustavo
Gutierrez or Hans Küng. The church as a whole must reflect the
vision of individuals such as these in racial, social and ecumenical affairs. While it may well need the vision and courage of the
individual to provide the initial inspiration, as was the case with
Ruth, in the long run that vision will be blurred unless it is taken
hold of and acted upon by the main body of believers.

CHAPTER 8

1 Samuel Chapter 17 Verse 45:
'Then David said to the Philistine,
"You come to me with a sword and with a spear and with a
javelin; but I come to you in the name of the Lord of hosts".'

Few stories in the bible are more dramatic than that of David's confrontation with Goliath. It has all the marks of a classic encounter; the underdog versus the strong favourite, youth versus experience, amateur verses professional, the reluctant shepherd boy verses the bellicose warrior. The details of the confrontation are well known as the giant Goliath crashes to defeat.

But the outcome was not always certain, as initially David went out to fight clothed with the heavy armour of King Saul which was more of a hindrance than a help. It was only when he shed the heavy armour and took his familiar sling in his hand and went out in the name of the Lord of hosts that he triumphed.

The right armour is important, and for the Christian this is set out clearly in the Letter to the Ephesians (6:13-18). There we have the familiar components of the armour of God systematically spelled out. But they are in fact to be found surfacing all over the New Testament because there is a consistency and constancy in the type of life the Christian is called to lead, involving truth, righteousness, peace, faith, prayer and the word of God. These do not alter from generation to generation.

However, from the story of David and Goliath we learn some deep, significant lessons about the use of armour.

(1) The first is that we must make the armour our own. When David came to the battlefield we read that 'Saul clothed David with his armour; he put a helmet of bronze on his head, and clothed him with a coat of mail.' One can imagine just how inhibited this free-running shepherd lad must have felt. 'He tried in vain to go, for he was not used to them.' And so he took them off and instead took his staff in his hand and chose five smooth stones from the brook.

What this is saying is that we must make the armour of God our own. We cannot live off other people's spiritual experience any more than we can live off the spirituality of other ages. We can gain inspiration from other people and from the past, but in the long run we must work out our own salvation in the sense that we will be personally responsible for our lives. 'Bear fruit worthy of repentance. Do not presume to say to yourselves, we have Abraham as our ancestor' (Mt 3:9).

(2) But the armour that David had was used expertly, and this was so because it was used often. As he guarded the sheep on the lonely hillside he often had to use his sling to protect and deliver them from the lions and bears. Therefore when the real crunch came he was proficient because his armour had been in constant use. So it is with the whole armour of God, with such elements as truth, peace, prayer and the word of God. If these are not our constant companions, the protection afforded by the whole armour of God will become less and less effective. David's armour was of use when it mattered because it was in constant use.

(3) In the third place, the armour of David was effective not just in itself, but it was appropriate for the task in hand, and therefore David had confidence in it. Despite the awesome appearance and power of the opposition, David was confident – 'This day the Lord will deliver you into my hand.'

There is a real need to rediscover this confidence in the armour of God, to reaffirm the priority of truth, righteousness and peace, and the efficacy of prayer and the word of God.

For David the adversary was clearly defined and very obvious in the person of Goliath. Today 'we are not contending against flesh and blood, but against principalities, against the powers, against the world rulers of this present darkness, against the spiritual hosts of wickedness in the heavenly place.' (Eph 6:12). The familiar words of the hymn (548 *Irish Church Hymnal*) remind us of what is required:

To keep your armour bright
Attend with constant care,
Still walking in your Captain's sight
And watching unto prayer.

CHAPTER 9

1 Kings Chapter 17 Verse 24:
'Now I know that you are a man of God,
and that the word of the Lord in your mouth is truth.'

One of the most remarkable men in the bible was Elijah. His appearance on the scene of history was sudden and dramatic. He is depicted as warning Ahab of a great famine that would strike the land, and subsequently he himself survived by drinking water from the brook Cherith and being fed by the widow at Zarephath.

Later he was involved in a famous confrontation with the prophets of Baal on Mount Carmel, while his denunciation of Ahab's wife Jezebel over the incident involving Naboth's vineyard proved to be prophetic as we read in 2 Kgs 9. Even Elijah's departure is dramatic as he was taken up by a whirlwind into heaven.

In the history of Israel, Elijah, the fearless prophet, is linked with Moses the great lawgiver, even though centuries separated them. It was as though the law given by Moses was taken afresh and applied anew to the life of the nation and its leaders by Elijah.

In the New Testament it was Moses and Elijah who appeared on the Mount of Transfiguration, and on the Cross Our Lord's cry, 'Eli, Eli, lama sabachthani' was interpreted by some as a cry for Elijah. It was a reminder of the esteem in which Elijah was held in Jewish thought. Even today a vacant chair is kept at Passover in readiness for his return. In looking at the life of Elijah, it becomes clear that he was someone raised up by God to combat the evil of heathenism in his day. Baal and Yahweh were mutually exclusive forces. In his day Elijah saw issues very clear cut. As one reads the latter half of 1 Kings, with its intrigue, double dealing and moral debauchery, there was obviously a need for this direct approach.

What of today? Can there be the same direct approach? If

Elijah was alive today he would no doubt be more direct than many of us are in relation to the moral and ethical issues that face society; marriage breakdown, divorce, premarital sex, drug abuse, alcoholism.

Yet however direct Elijah might be if he was alive today, his attitude would have to be conditioned by the revelation of God in Jesus Christ. 'Let this mind be in you which was also in Christ Jesus' was the way St Paul put it, and this principle must direct the Christian at all times.

But how does one seek the mind of Christ? There are no short cuts, but the time-honoured methods are available to all – meditation on the life of Christ, the reading of scripture, the use of our own faculty of reason, prayer, a consideration of history and tradition, and not least through the testing of our views in the open forum of discussion. It is only as we struggle and agonise in these ways that we come to understand, however dimly, an outline of the mind of Christ. It cannot be said too often that Our Lord did not pontificate on specific issues, but left principles very often enshrined in simple stories such as The Prodigal Son and The Good Samaritan.

Perhaps as we struggle with today's complex ethical and social issues, what is required is a merging of the two approaches, the directness of Elijah to point up the inherent evil in the world, and the mind of Christ to deal compassionately with those caught in the consequent tangled web.

CHAPTER 10

2 Kings Chapter 5 Verse 25:
'He went in, and stood before his master, and Elisha said to
him, "Where have you been, Gehazi?"
And he said, "Your servant went nowhere."'

Naaman, the commander of the army of the king of Syria, had
been healed of his leprosy. It is a story with a happy ending, one
of the best known in the Old Testament.

However, its sequel, involving Elisha's servant Gehazi, had
not such a happy ending. By means of subterfuge, involving a
series of lies, he received from Naaman money and clothing.
When confronted by Elisha he tried to cover up: 'Your servant
went nowhere.' But Elisha was not to be deceived and the conse-
quence for Gehazi was that the leprosy of Naaman passed to
him and he went out from the presence of his master 'a leper, as
white as snow'.

Leaving aside the moral consideration involved in breaking
the ninth commandment, 'You shall not bear false witness
against your neighbour,' the story of Gehazi is a vivid example
of the tangle that develops once a person goes down the road of
untruth.

It all began in verse 22 with the fabricated story of the two
young men who had come to visit Elisha and the request for
gifts to give them. But once that avenue of deceit was opened up
there was no turning back. When faced with Elisha's question,
'Where have you been Gehazi?', there was a certain inevitability
about the reply, 'Your servant went nowhere.' But Elisha knew
differently. 'Did I not go with you in spirit when the man turned
from his chariot to meet you?' The result was tragedy for Gehazi
as he went out from the presence of Elisha 'a leper, as white as
snow'.

It is a sorry tale, but one not uncommon in society. A tale of
misplaced trust brought into even sharper focus as the person
involved was operating within a religious context. Elisha was a

prophet of God and there would have been an expectation of integrity from those closest to him.

But the religious context is no guarantee of ethical integrity. Even Judas Iscariot, despite his membership of the apostolic band and his closeness to Our Lord, was not immune, and his betrayal of his Master is a constant reminder of the frailty of human nature, an unfortunate fact, as true today as at any other time in history.

CHAPTER 11

1 Chronicles Chapter 29 Verse 11:
'Thine, O Lord, is the greatness, and the power, and the glory, and the victory, and the majesty.'

Have you ever listened to a piece of music and said, 'I know that tune well, but just can't think of its name.' It can be a mildly frustrating experience.

It can also happen with familiar quotations from the bible. It certainly happens to the preacher who may want to use a particular text but, without a concordance, spends much time searching for its origin.

One such quotation is that used Sunday by Sunday in churches up and down the country when the offertory is being received. It is a familiar quotation repeated with conviction by many congregations, but how many are aware that it comes from the depths of the Old Testament, from the comparatively little used book, 1 Chronicles, and that it had its origin in words of David as he blessed the Lord?

The whole quotation can be divided into three sections: an affirmation (verse 11), a thanksgiving (verse 13) and a response (verse 14b).

(1) 'Thine, O Lord, is the greatness, and the power, and the glory, and the victory, and the majesty; for all that is in the heavens and in the earth is thine; thine is the kingdom, O Lord, and thou art exalted as head above all.'

This is a wonderful affirmation to lift the drooping spirit in time of depression.

Despite their position near the beginning of the bible, the Books of Chronicles are believed to have been written after the exile of Israel in Babylon. It was a traumatic experience. All the hopes of the Children of Israel lay shattered. Their confidence in God was at its lowest point. How could he have allowed his chosen people to come to such at state?

Yet despite all these setbacks and the apparent neglect by

God, their belief and confidence were never completely eroded, and they found expression in these magnificent words from 1 Chronicles.

As we look around on the world today with its catalogue of tragedies we constantly need to be reassured that God is in control, that the forces of evil will not triumph. The affirmation from Chronicles can stimulate that assurance. But because we live, not just after the exile, but also after the resurrection, we can have that double assurance which comes from the knowledge that God has acted decisively in history and we shall overcome because he has overcome. In the resurrection of Jesus Christ there is not just hope but the proof of ultimate victory.

(2) The affirmation of the greatness of God is followed by the thanksgiving: 'And now we thank thee, our God, and praise thy glorious name.' This should be a natural outcome. Thanksgiving should be a regular part of our prayers, not just in private but in public also, not just thanksgiving for blessings, but for the whole involvement of God in human affairs.

Again, because we live not just after the exile but after the resurrection, we have a special reason for thanksgiving. Nowhere is this summed up better than in the words of a General Thanksgiving: 'We bless you for our creation and preservation and for all the blessings of this life; but above all for your love in redeeming the world by our Lord Jesus Christ.' We thank God not just because of his power, majesty and glory; not just because all that is in the earth and heaven is his; but especially for the redemption wrought by Jesus Christ of which the resurrection is a sure sign.

(3) After the affirmation and the thanksgiving comes the response. In one sense, our thanksgiving through prayer is our response. But the writer of Chronicles goes a practical step further (verse 14). 'For all things come from thee, and of thine own have we given thee.'

In the Old Testament one of the fundamental beliefs that finds expression over and over again is that the earth is the Lord's and all that is in it. This is carried over into the New

Testament and underlined in a parable such as 'the talents.' We are stewards while here on earth who will one day be answerable to God for our use or abuse of that selfsame earth. 'Turn in the account of your stewardship' (Lk 16:2) is the challenge that will be put to each one of us.

Week by week, when we use the familiar words from First Chronicles, we are not only affirming with thankfulness the sovereignty of God, we are acknowledging that what we are offering to God is in reality his own. But even more than this. Through our offering of money we are in fact offering ourselves in his service. At the offertory in the Holy Communion this becomes very obvious. The bread and wine symbolise the work of our hands, while the money collected symbolises ourselves, our souls and bodies.

Each Sunday as we witness the offering being brought to the Lord's Table, and as we hear the familiar words said over them, we should be aware that it is not just a subscription to a club we are making, but the offering to God of what is his own and the re-dedication of ourselves in his service.

CHAPTER 12

Job Chapter 28 Verses 12 and 28:
'But where shall wisdom be found?'
'Behold the fear of the Lord, that is wisdom.'

Where shall wisdom be found? Such was the question posed by Job. In the succeeding verses the writer goes on to point out the difficulty of attaining wisdom, or spiritual insight into the affairs of the world. To be sure man has knowledge of a kind – 'He binds up the streams that they do not trickle' (28:11); 'He cuts out channels in the rocks' (28:10). But this type of knowledge is not true wisdom.

'Whence then comes wisdom?' the writer asks, and he gives the answer in the very last verse of the chapter, 'Behold, the fear of the Lord, that is wisdom.'

Yet the bible speaks of the fear of the Lord as something very worthwhile, indeed as an essential part of our spiritual lives.

But what do we mean by fear as it is used in the bible? Basically it relates to reverence for God arising out of the realisation of God's power.

In the Christian faith we ponder very often on the love of God. The Christian faith owes its very existence to the fact of God's love revealing itself supremely in Jesus Christ. 'Love came down at Christmas.'

But side by side with the concept of the love of God we must place the idea of the power of God. Not that love and power are to be thought of as incompatible or mutually exclusive. There is, after all, no more powerful force than love in the world, whether it be in terms of individual or corporate relationships.

However, in the Old Testament it is the thought of God's power in a regal, almost secular sense, that is emphasised. Love is there, as in the story of Hosea. But it is not the dominant theme, it is in the background. The Children of Israel were rescued from Egypt, but the whole incident, with its many signs and wonders, seems calculated to vindicate God's power rather than his love. It is from this fact of God's power that reverence arises, or 'fear', used in its biblical sense.

We may sometimes feel that the power of God is over-stressed in the Old Testament, and certainly the crude exercise of power reflected, for example, in the mass annihilation of Israel's enemies in the time of Saul and David, has done little to commend the Father of Our Lord Jesus Christ. But in our efforts to redress the balance we must not eliminate the notion altogether, and this is a danger today. In making God presentable to modern minds the notion of a powerful God is in danger of being eliminated, and with it the obligation to display reverence. God has been described recently as a benevolent grandfather, and in less laudable terms as a divine sugar-daddy.

Yet if we take the overall picture of God in the Old Testament this is far from being the case. Moses walked with reverence before God at the burning bush, and on Mount Sinai he had to hide his face. It is of the wicked that the psalmist can write, 'there is no fear of God before his eyes' (Ps 36:1).

Turning to the New Testament where we have in Jesus the image of the invisible God, reverence is still a part of the context. The picture is of a leader for whom his followers had great respect. Even those not of the inner circle used the reverential term 'Rabbi', while at the conclusion of the Sermon on the Mount the crowds recognised that 'he taught them as one who had authority.'

Today there are signs that reverence for God is diminishing. The erosion of Sunday, however rationalised, is an indication of this, as is the need to keep churches closed because of vandalism. At another level, erosion has been hastened by the spate of well-publicised clerical scandals. The clerical pedestal is no longer as secure as once it was believed to be. While all this may boost the sales of the tabloids it does nothing to safeguard that reverence for God or fear of the Lord, which is at the heart of true spirituality.

'Where shall wisdom be found?' That is the question at the centre of all spiritual striving. To the age old question comes back the age old reply, 'Behold the fear of the Lord, that is wisdom.'

CHAPTER 13

Psalm 95 Verse 1:
'O come, let us sing to the Lord.'

I once attended a meeting of clergy and organists where one of the organists passed the comment that if he had to choose between leaving out the hymns or the psalm from a service he would choose to leave out the hymns. To many of us, who were used to singing hymns as an integral part of church services, this sounded rather strange.

However, as it transpired it was less a denigration of the hymn book and more an indication of the affection and esteem in which the Psalter is held by many people. It also reminded us of the place the psalms have held in the life of the church and individual Christians down through the centuries. For example, the Psalter was known as the Prayer Book of Our Lord because of the use he made of it, and like all Jewish boys of his day he would have been steeped in its contents and able to quote freely from it.

Again, in early monastic days the psalms were learnt by heart and used by the monks on all possible occasions at their work. It was in some words from Psalm 84 that the monastic vocation came to St Thomas Aquinas – 'I would rather be a doorkeeper in the house of my God than dwell in the tents of wickedness' (v 10).

The psalms were Jewish in origin and we must never forget the debt we owe to the Jewish people for this treasury of devotion. Over the years they have been incorporated into Christian worship and in a real sense have become Christianised.

We can think of a psalm in two ways – its original meaning and its later application. To turn again to Psalm 84, this is what is know as a pilgrim psalm. The writer appears to be on a pilgrim journey to Jerusalem. His thoughts are set on the temple, the focal point of Judaism. It is before the exile in Babylon, that very traumatic event, when the temple was devastated and the hope of the Jews was at its lowest ebb. But as yet there was no reason to have anything but joyful anticipation – 'Blessed are those who dwell in

thy house, ever singing thy praise' (v 4). Even though times might
be difficult, yet at Jerusalem in the temple all would be well. The
vale of misery would be transformed by the presence of the God
of gods in Zion. There is no more explicit expression of loyalty
and commitment than the words already quoted from verse 10.
Even the most lowly task in the temple, the doorkeeper, was to be
cherished above all else.

On the other hand, in the Christian context this psalm has been
often used as a form of preparation for Holy Communion. The
Christian too is on a pilgrimage. As he goes through life he is sustained by the grace of God which is so often experienced at the
altar of God in the House of God. Our thoughts are turned in this
direction as we read verse 3:

Even the sparrow finds a home,

And the swallow a nest for herself,

Where she may lay her young,

At thy altars, O Lord of hosts,

My King and my God.

The whole psalm points to the joy of worship and the strength
that comes from the encounter with God.

In a sense the key to the Christian understanding of the psalm
is found in the very last verse: 'O Lord of hosts, blessed is the man
who trusts in thee.' The Christian knows, as the Old Testament
psalmist could not have known, that his trust in God is not misplaced. God has proved his faithfulness by what Christ has done
for us, by taking upon himself the sin of the world. And so, in the
context of Christian devotion, a psalm such as this takes on a new
dimension. When we add the Gloria at the end of a psalm it is not
a mere empty formula, but a reminder that the high ideals and as-
pirations of the psalm have found fulfilment in Christ.

Our organist friend, who valued the psalms so highly that he
was prepared to trade the hymnal for them if necessary, was
probably exceptional. But at the same time he was drawing our
attention to a very remarkable devotional heritage which, not just
in the context of Jewish worship, but also in terms of Christian
worship, has stood the most severe test of all – the test of time.

CHAPTER 14

Psalm 24 Verse 1:
'The earth is the Lord's and the fulness thereof.'

When the history of the latter part of the twentieth century comes to be written, there is no doubt that one word will occupy a leading place, and that word is 'environment'. Today the world at large has become environmentally conscious in a way that was hardly imaginable even twenty years ago.

Governments now have departments and ministers of the environment; political parties have sprung up devoted to the cause of the environment; reprocessing plants ensure that environmentally friendly products are recycled; those with this interest at heart are willing to risk life and limb and freedom for the protection of the environment. Indeed there is scarcely a day goes by but the media offers an article or programme on some aspect of the environment.

There are no doubt good reasons for this interest in the environment. There is, for example, a recognition that what is happening in places such as Brazil and British Columbia, where forests are being denuded of trees, is having a disastrous effect on the climate generally. The graphic pictures of oil slicks which are brought to us at intervals from different locations throughout the world underline one of the environmental hazards of modern society. While we may not all understand the technicalities of the greenhouse effect, we are none the less aware that the style of living of modern society is having a serious effect on the atmosphere as global warming increases. At the local level, there is continuing concern for the state of Cork harbour, while the fiftieth anniversary of the dropping of the atomic bombs, and the Chernobyl Children's project, are sad reminders of the environmental hazards which scientific advances bring in their wake.

The environment is an emotive subject and recognised as such by our church authorities. At the Lambeth Conference in 1988 it was debated with vigour and discussed even though it was overshadowed in the media by other issues such as violence and the ordination of women. Part of Resolution 40 referred to 'irreversible damage to the environment' and called on each province and diocese 'actively to support, by public statement and private dialogue, the engagement of governments, transnational corporations, management and labour in an examination of what their decisions are doing to our people, and our land, air and water.'

This places an onus on each one of us not only to engage our public representatives in dialogue on this matter but to support them when they act for the good of the environment.

But not only did the Lambeth Conference devote much attention to this issue. The Church of Ireland at the General Synod has also had it high on its agenda. In 1987 (European Environmental Year) major comment was made by the Role of the Church Committee, and this was actually taken up by the Anglican Consultative Council and used as a basis for discussion on world environmental problems at its meeting in Singapore the same year. It is a subject which has received attention every year since, in one form or another, because there is not a year passes without some new threat to the environment, whether it be at the local, national or international level.

Why then should the Christian have this keen concern for the environment?

In the first place, it is bound up with the fundamental affirmation of the psalmist – 'The earth is the Lord's and the fulness thereof.' The earth is God's gift to humanity and anything that threatens the earth threatens God's gift. In the opening chapter of the bible (Gen 1:28) we read of God's blessing, 'Be fruitful and multiply, and fill the earth and subdue it.' How often has the earth been subdued without recognising the complementary responsibility? Power without responsibility in any sphere of life can lead to the most dangerous excesses. It is this danger which has led one modern writer (Denis Carrol, *Ethics and the Christian*, p 128) to comment rather cynically: 'Here at the very commencement of the bible the licence of despoilation seems to be conceded

... Destruction, competition and cruelty receive a compliant wink.' A more balanced comment is that of Alan Richardson, in his *Torch Bible Commentary on Genesis* (p 55). 'But man must remember that he is lord of creation and ruler of nature not in his own right or to work his own will; he is God's viceregent, charged with the working of God's will, responsible to God for his stewardship. Otherwise his science and industry will bring not a blessing but a curse; they will make of the earth not a paradise but a dust bowl or a Hiroshima.' The key word is stewardship. We are stewards of God's creation, bearing an ultimate responsibility to the Creator.

In the second place, the Christian has an interest in the environment because he believes that in some sense, not fully understood, creation has been redeemed and has a place in God's redemptive purposes. 'God was in Christ reconciling the world to himself.' Here and there in the New Testament we have what have been described as 'occasional and tantalising glimpses of cosmic implications' (*Role of the Church Report 1987*). Perhaps the clearest expression of this is to be found in Romans 8:21 – 'the creation itself will be set free from its bondage to decay and obtain the glorious liberty of the children of God.'

While we may not fully understand what these words mean, they surely lead us to take seriously our care for the environment lest we find ourselves working against the purposes of God. It is, after all, the Christian's calling to be a fellow worker with God in the farmyard of creation. It is not without significance that the theme of the 7th Assembly of the World Council of Churches was 'Come Holy Spirit – Renew the Whole Creation.'

Thirdly, the Christian has an interest in the environment because he has a concern for the well-being of humanity as a whole. The Christian is his brother's and his sister's keeper. Much of the suffering through hunger in the world is caused by a misuse of the environment and that is why educational and development projects are so vital in the Third World context. The need for instant relief so often claims the headlines, but hand in hand with this must go longterm development of the environment, leading to self-sufficency. It is this balance which the committee of the Bishops' Appeal (the Church of Ireland's Relief and Development Fund) seeks to maintain as it allocates money to projects worldwide.

Some words from a prayer by a Scots Presbyterian, John Baillie, point to the attitude which should be ours as we contemplate the world around us:

Creator Spirit:

Forbid that I should walk through thy beautiful world with unseeing eyes.

Forbid that the lure of the market place should ever entirely steal my heart away from

the love of the open areas and the green trees;

Forbid that under the low roof of workshop or office or study I should ever forget

thy overarching sky.

Let the energy and vigour which in thy wisdom Thou hast infused into every living thing

stir today within my being;

that I may not be among thy creatures as a sluggard or a drone;

And above all give me grace to use these beauties of earth without me and this eager

stirring within me as means whereby my soul may rise from creature to Creator,

and from nature to nature's God.

Yes! 'The earth is the Lord's and the fulness thereof.' Although culled from the Old Testament, these words contain a fundamental Christian principle. Once we accept it we then must see ourselves as responsible stewards of the environment, as fellow workers with God in redeeming and maintaining the environment in order that it may meet the needs of humanity.

CHAPTER 15

Proverbs Chapter 1 Verse 1:
'The proverbs of Solomon, son of David, king of Israel.'

'The wisdom of Solomon' is an expression which is common-place today, and a very good illustration of how the language and thought of the bible have been incorporated into everyday speech.

In 1 Kgs 4:32 Solomon is said to have spoken three thousand proverbs. By these were meant originally popular sayings such as are found among all communities. They are generally short and direct, and contain some advice or warning which is of a practical nature. Ireland abounds in comparable sayings, and there is not a district but can boast of such a catalogue.

Similar sayings characterise the Book of Proverbs. The core of the book (chapters 10-22) and the proverbs in this section are all assigned to Solomon. No doubt he uttered many wise sayings, but no doubt many more were attributed to him because of his reputation. Again, a number of proverbs were probably gathered from the surrounding countries. There is a pool of wisdom and ideas from which we all draw.

When we read the Book of Proverbs, one of its values is that it gives an insight into some of the ordinary ideas that guided the Hebrew people. Running through the book there is a lofty code of conduct and a high ethical ideal. The book provides what has been described as a healthy check to extreme other-worldliness.

Yet when we read the Book of Proverbs we must exercise care. Its practical precepts are those of a people who had yet not moved far forward in their spiritual pilgrimage. Although there is a high ethical standard portrayed, there is a certain lack of tenderness and sympathy. One is reminded of Mr Worldly Wiseman in *The Pilgrim's Progress,* who always goes to the town of morality to church, whose religion is equated with respectability.

But this falls far short of the spiritual level of the New Testament. There we move to a more embracing level of conduct. All that is contained in Proverbs still applies, but there is a much greater challenge presented, the challenge of the Cross worked out in sacrifice, service and sympathy. There is movement away from concern for one's personal, practical contentment, to a loving concern for others.

Typical of the ethical exhortation in Proverbs is chapter 16, verse 17: 'The highway of the upright turns aside from evil; he who guards his way preserves his life.' But does this challenge the reader in a vital way? And even if it does, it leaves him struggling and striving alone?

We need more than ethical exhortations no matter how graphically they are presented, and some are contained in very picturesque language, for example chapter 26, verse 22: 'The words of a whisperer are like delicious morsels; they go down into the inner parts of the body.' We need a living example and the assurance of the grace of God. These we have in Jesus Christ. As our example he has shown us that the true way of life is that of sacrifice, service and sympathy. In response to John the Baptist's question from prison, he says to John's followers: 'Go and tell John what you hear and see; the blind receive their sight and the lame walk, lepers are cleansed and the deaf hear, and the dead are raised up, and the poor have good news preached to them' (Mt 11:4-5). In other words, at the heart of the Christian way of life is this practical element following the example of Our Lord.

But there must be more than mere example, mere exhortation. There must be strength and power which are found in the presence of him who said, 'Lo, I am with you always' (Mt 28:20), and reflected in the words of the well known hymn 'Fight the good fight with all they might! Christ is thy strength and Christ thy right.' Without his presence the exhortations of Proverbs and the challenge of his own example become burdens grievous to be borne. But in the strength of his presence they become beacons on the spiritual pilgrimage.

CHAPTER 16

Ecclesiastes Chapter 5 Verse 12:
'Sweet is the sleep of a labourer.'

In these words from Ecclesiastes is summed up one of the fundamental truths of humanity, that man was created to work as a
means of fulfilment and is most contented when he is working.
This is why unemployment is such a scourge of society in that it
takes the real purpose out of life and diminishes a person's essential dignity. The words from Ecclesiastes come from a male-
dominated era, and while the role of women in the workplace is
an accepted fact today, it would often appear that the stigma of
unemployment weighs most heavily on a man.

It is on Rogation Sunday that the church directs its thoughts
and prayers to the subject of work. This particular observance
has a long history, dating from 470 AD when a bishop in France
ordered special prayers to be said after a failure of crops. This
gradually became a regular feature of church life – to pray for
God's blessing on the sowing of the seeds. Basically Rogation
simply means asking, in this case asking a blessing on the crops.

However, a new dimension has been added in recent years
reflecting a shift in society, so that in many places the title now
used is Rogation and Industrial Sunday.

In the nineteenth century, the Industrial Revolution in
England brought about a change in the whole structure of society. This was eventually reflected in Ireland, particularly in the
North of Ireland. In the town of Newtownards in Co Down in
the early fifties there were no less that forty-eight factories. The
industrial estates to be found in the outskirts of many cities and
towns in the South of Ireland indicate how far the Republic has
caught up in this matter.

Because of this new factor, Industrial Sunday was first ob-
served in 1920 and was the initial major event in the programme
of the newly formed Industrial Christian Fellowship in Belfast,
which was representative of all the main line churches including

the Roman Catholic. In order to assist the Church of Ireland in its understanding of the problems of industry, an industrial officer was appointed in the 1950s. The constraints of finance, rather than a diminution of need, were to lead to the eventual withdrawal of the post .

With the linking of Rogation Sunday and Industrial Sunday, the Church of Ireland has adapted a long-standing custom to present day conditions so that we now have a day when we not only pray for God's blessing on the crops but also on all our work which we offer anew to God.

In relation to work in general, two points can be made from a Christian perspective.

The first relates to the quality of work. The Christian seeks to observe certain standards in all activities, such standards as honesty, truthfulness and charity. Because life is a unit in which all aspects are interrelated, these standards should apply in work as well as home and recreation and the many other relationships people develop. Work is not an exclusive area of life where different rules apply. The guideline which has almost become a household phrase is 'an honest day's work for an honest day's pay.'

It is not just the spoken word but the quality of the Christian's work which bears witness to the faith. The faith worked out in everyday situations is a real part of the work of the church, and with the competitive pressures of the modern workplace many would say that it is the most difficult part of the church's work. How true were the words of William Temple that 'nine-tenths of the work of the church in the world is done by Christian people fulfilling responsibilities and performing tasks which in themselves are not part of the official system of the church at all.'

The Christian faith is illustrated most eloquently, not necessarily in the exhortations of leaders, but in the life and work of the rank and file. All too readily people look for official pronouncements, imagining that these relieve them of responsibility. It is one of the hopeful signs of more recent church life that the nature of the church as community is being rediscovered, in which the Christian Faith must be worked out by all members in all situations. This includes the workplace with all its tensions, frustrations and monotony as well at its joy, happiness and fulfilment.

The second point concerns the offering of our work to God.

We see our work in a new light if we regard it as an offering to God, part of our service to and worship of him. In offering our work to God we see it more clearly as part of our total life which is committed to him.

For most people their work is what really matters in life. By means of it they earn a living, support themselves and their families, and find a sense of purpose. If this is not offered to God then religion becomes a very stunted affair and reserved for the non-essential areas of life, a pastime in which to dabble. In these circumstances the church is viewed as a club of likeminded individuals who come together for a type of relaxation when the hard chores of the day are completed. It is this attitude which gives substance to Chesterton's doggerel verse: 'A Christian is a man who feels repentance on a Sunday for what he's done on Saturday and is going to do on Monday.' It is only as work is offered to him who is Lord of Lords and King of Kings that reality and relevance are brought back into faith. This is highlighted at the offertory in the Communion Service where the bread and the wine symbolise the work of people's hands which is then offered and later received back, blessed for God's service.

In less dramatic form, time spent in church, especially each Sunday, can be used as an opportunity for the re-dedication of one's work during the coming week.

The quality of work and the attitude in the workplace should be affected by being offered to God. This is the important truth of which we are reminded each year on Rogation Sunday.

CHAPTER 17

Isaiah Chapter 30 Verses 15 and 16:
'For thus said the Lord God, the Holy one of Israel,
in returning and rest you shall be saved;
in quietness and in trust shall be your strength.
And you would not, but you said, No!
We will speed upon horses, therefore you shall speed away,
and we will ride upon swift steeds,
therefore your pursuers shall be swift.'

At times in parish life we are all left breathless, as one event follows hard on the heels of another. Now, to be continually engaged in doing, to be caught up in the activity syndrome, is not only exhausting physically, it drains one mentally and spiritually as well. And so it is important that the balance of parish life be constantly checked. Not that we should cease altogther from doing, but that we do not neglect to wait upon the Lord.

Let me illustrate what I mean from two sources I encountered during the past week.

The first is part of a reading from Isaiah, and is the text I have chosen. It speaks of both quietness and speed.

Most of us, if we are honest, are happier, metaphorically speaking, on horses and swift steeds than in rest and quietness. Yet the challenging words from Isaiah are, 'in returning and rest you shall be saved, and in quietness and in trust shall be your strength', a truth emphasised elsewhere in Isaiah (40:31): 'they who wait for the Lord shall renew their strength, they shall mount up with wings like eagles, they shall run and not be weary, they shall walk and not faint.'

The second source was a letter I received recently from a friend in Sri Lanka. Ratna is a schoolteacher in India, one of whose sisters is an Anglican nun in an enclosed order in England. Her letters are the type one keeps and rereads with profit. After some comment on the turbulent political scene, she went on: 'As for me, I am happy at my work. I am far too busy to do what I often long to do – to read. I have been very interested in reading what Mother Julian and others, like the writer of the *Cloud of Unknowing*, have to say about knowing God – not knowing about him. Yet I know that the life of the contemplative is not for me. I don't know why I feel that. When I look back on my life I can see I have tried, at least, to keep on doing what I thought was God's will for my days, but somehow I don't know him – except at times. I have so far been content but I am increasingly not so. Maybe I long for and desire what is not to be mine. I am not unhappy, just puzzled. I continue praying, reading, thinking and hoping that God will give me both knowledge and love to know him in fact.'

Many of us are happy to remain at the point of knowing *about* God, and Christmas is a time when, in a strange way, this is emphasised as we hear over and over again the old old story. But knowing about God is only a stage, albeit an important stage, on the spiritual pilgrimage. The ultimate experience is to know God. For many the words of Ratna ring very true to life: 'I continue praying, reading, thinking and hoping that God will give me both knowledge and love to know him in fact.'

'In quietness and trust shall be your strength' is the assurance of scripture. 'I continue praying, reading and thinking' is the experience of a deeply spiritual individual. These two thoughts can help direct our lives so that in the process of time we will come to a deeper knowledge of God.

CHAPTER 18

Jeremiah Chapter 1 Verse 5:
'Before I formed you in the womb I knew you.'

One of the dominant figures at the 1988 Lambeth Conference was Archbishop Desmond Tutu. He is a complex character, presenting a many-sided personality. Through the media he is portrayed as a protesting political figure; very much a public figure not afraid to risk his life, who sees his loyalty to God as paramount.

But there is another side, a more private side. It manifests itself in his leading of retreats and in his meditation on the Word of God.

It was this other side of Desmond Tutu that delegates experienced one evening at the Lambeth Conference when he conducted a meditation for a packed and expectant gathering of thirteen hundred people, based on the opening words of the Bible: 'In the beginning God ...'

First of all, by skillful use of the images of God found in the bible, of one high and lifted up, of one worshipped by angels and archangels, he created a portrait of God in all his glory, splendour and power. It was a picture that reflected the opening words of the opening prayer of the conference itself: 'Eternal God, your greatness is beyond our understanding.'

But then, as we meditated on this exalted image of God, we were reminded, almost by way of contrast, of the love of God for each individual. For Desmond Tutu this was highlighted by the words from Jeremiah: 'Now the word of the Lord came to me saying, Before I formed you in the womb I knew you, and before you were born I consecrated you; I appointed you a prophet to the nations.'

Those who heard him repeat those words of scripture in his slow distinctive style will not easily forget the experience. He was speaking against a background of terrible injustice in South Africa where so much that was inhuman was taking place, including imprisonments, separation of families and murders.

All this being perpetrated against those who are children of God and of value in his sight.

It is this realisation that gives dignity to those who are so often treated with disdain. It was this realisation that impelled the Christian churches in South Africa to give a lead in the fight against apartheid which they regarded as blasphemy, and moved church leaders to risk their lives.

But the words from Jeremiah move us a stage further. We go on to read: 'Before you were born I consecrated you' or set you apart. Why was Jeremiah set apart? It was to be 'a prophet to the nations.'

There was a contemporary ring about those words when one thought of the church leaders in South Africa and the role they were playing. A little further on, the same contemporary element can again be found: 'To all to whom I send you you shall go, and whatever I command you you shall speak. Be not afraid of them, for I am with you to deliver you, said the Lord.'

It was this command, coupled with this assurance, that compelled leaders such as Desmond Tutu to keep on speaking and protesting.

At Lambeth, those present became vividly aware that the situation in South Africa was not unique in terms of persecution as they heard of what was happening in other parts of Africa and Central and South America. A passing aside helps to illustrate the point. Sitting beside a bishop from Chile early on in the Conference as we voted on a minor procedural matter, his comment was 'that is the first time I have voted in fifteen years'.

But on the night in question the focus was on South Africa, and for those who heard the archbishop use the words from Jeremiah they will for ever have a special significance. 'Before I formed you in the womb I knew you, and before you were born I consecrated you.'

CHAPTER 19

Jeremiah Chapter 15 Verse 19:
'Therefore thus says the Lord:
"If you return, I will restore you, and you shall stand before me.
If you utter what is precious, and not what is worthless,
you shall be as my mouth.
They shall turn to you, but you shall not turn to them".'

These words are graphically interpreted in the Good News Bible: 'If instead of talking nonsense you proclaim a worthwhile message, you will be my prophet again. The people will come back to you ...'

During the next three days at the General Synod here in Cork, there will be much talking. Time alone will tell how much of it will be nonsense. But we must be careful in our judgment, because the foolishness of God, divine nonsense, confounds the wisdom of the wise, and what the world counts as gain may not always be equated with heavenly treasure: 'What does it profit a man if he gain the whole world and lose his own soul?' To many Good Friday was nonsense: 'To the Jews a stumbling block and to the Greeks foolishness.'

This is not to be taken as advocating a free rein to idiosyncratic orators, because at the end of the day what people will look for from us in our deliberations is a worthwhile message, just as they look for a worthwhile message from the church at large. But what are the marks of a worthwhile message? What are the criteria we should use in judging whether or not the church's message is authentic?

(1) First and foremost it must be God-centred, and it must relate to the God revealed in Jesus Christ.

Today there are gods many and lords many, ranging from the subtle, often quasi-medical expressions of the New Age Movement, for which parts of this diocese are noted, to the insidious tenets of consumerism which trade on the weaknesses of human nature, not least through the subtlety of advertising.

But the God whose kingdom the church exists to promote, and of which the church itself must be a foretaste, is the God of whom Our Lord could say: 'I and the Father are one.'

And so we must look to proclaim the kingdom values which were revealed in Jesus Christ and outlined for example by St Paul: 'Whatever is true, honourable, just, pure, lovely, gracious.' These values must be self-evident in the life of the church. How else can we hope to preach a credible gospel to the world? Canon Samuel van Culin, outgoing Secretary of the Anglican Communion, in his introduction to the report of the 1993 Cape Town meeting of the Anglican Consultative Council, puts the matter succinctly: 'the vision must be of a church, alive and working to bring God's kingdom to fulfilment.'

But is all this so very different from what was being said at the General Synod thirty years ago? Then we were being called not to a Decade of Evangelism but to a Responsibility Year. Perhaps the church was not as chronologically ambitious in those days. But listen to what was said by the then Primate, a man with an underrated practical and prophetic voice, unfortunate to be sandwiched between two of the giants of the Church of Ireland, Archbishops Gregg and Simms. Speaking at the General Synod in 1964, Dr James McCann said: 'Perhaps the evangelism should begin with ourselves. Do these our brethren for whom we are concerned see in us a better example of charity and kindness, simplicity of living and rejection of material values because of our churchmanship? Do we present the image of Christian Fellowship to them? Do we stand for moral principles and standards of behaviour in daily living that are distinctive?' Thirty years on these are still challenging words.

The church's message to be worthwhile must be God-centred.

(2) In the second place, it must be experiential.

To be a confident message in the face of many conflicting ideologies it must derive from experience of the power of the Holy Spirit. 'Say not we have Abraham to our Father.' It is so easy for us as a church with deep historical roots to live off the past, to feed off the spiritual crumbs that fall from the table of past generations. We thank God for all that has been true and good in the lives of our forefathers, for the inspiration they have been and the example they have left us. But we must be ourselves and allow the Holy Spirit to guide us, to move us on. 'The great thing in this world', said a famous American President (Holmes), 'is not so much where we stand as in what direction we are moving.'

(3) And this leads on directly to the third mark of an authentic message. It must be relevant. It must be capable to being applied and worked out in the cauldron of today's society.

Of course, this is no new thought. Three years ago, our Primate in his presidential address, challenged us in a very direct way: 'The question we should be asking constantly as we consider the life of the Church of Ireland is "Is it relevant to what we are called to be and to do?"'

There was a time when we as a church tended to stand apart, some would say aloof, from society. Historically it may well have been the only way to survive. But today the context is radically different. Today there is evidence that the voice of the minority in the South of Ireland is being heard and heeded, not in any gratuitous way, but because it is recognised as an authentic voice with a message that is essential to the well-being of society. Slowly but surely it is being realised that diversity of opinion must be tolerated if maturity is to mean anything.

In this situation we are called to address the issues of the day, whether they be social, political, or ethical; whether they affect the starving millions of the Third World, the peace process on this island, or the cancer of unemployment so evident in parts of this city. Unless we are addressing these issues we will be regarded as irrelevant, and rightly so.

This does not necessarily mean that we as a church have to set up our own structures. Often it means playing our part in organisations already in existence, both statutory and voluntary, and there is evidence that this is happening more and more. Where it does happen it is valued and appreciated perhaps more than we fully understand.

(4) This is not to deny the need on occasions for an identifiable minority voice, especially in ethical issues. And this leads on to a fourth mark of a worthwhile message – it must be compassionate.

One would need to read the gospel accounts with very blinkered eyes not to appreciate the compassion of Jesus Christ and his concern for the marginalised of society, including the sinners he encountered. There are few more telling scenes in the bible than that of the woman brought to Jesus caught in the act of adultery, and his handling of the situation by confronting her accusers with their own sinfulness, until eventually they had all left. Jesus looked and said to her, 'Woman where are they? Has no one condemned you?' She said, 'No one Lord.' And Jesus said, 'Neither do I condemn you; go, and do not sin again.'

It is Edmond Browning, Presiding Bishop of the Episcopal Church in the United States of America, who consistently insists that the church be a place where there are 'no outcasts.' But it can only be that type of place if it exercises compassion. Not the type of compassion which has as a sub-title 'anything goes', but the type of compassion that reflects the mind of Christ when he said, 'Neither do I condemn you; go, and do not sin again.'

During the coming months, or perhaps over a longer period, here in the South of Ireland we will have an opportunity to put our compassion to the test as we are faced with a divorce referendum. Somewhere in the midst of all the rhetoric, and there will be plenty of it you can be sure, there must be evidence of compassion for the many caught up in the tragedy of broken marriage if our Christian profession is to mean anything other than a slavish adherence to pre-selected positions. It was William Temple, one of the great Archbishops of Canterbury, who once said: 'It is possible to be morally right repulsively', which is perhaps another way of saying with St Paul that the letter kills but the spirit gives life. Without compassion we can scarcely claim to be imitators of Christ.

(5) No catalogue of criteria regarding the church's message, no matter how selective or arbitrary, would be complete without one more. It must be ecumenical.

Hans Küng, who packed this Cathedral not so many years ago, wrote recently that 'to be a real Christian is to be an ecumenical Christian' The rule of Taizé, that remarkable ecumenical institution which attracts so many people each year, not least young people, impressionable young people, says 'never resign yourself to the scandal of the separation of Christians ... be consumed with burning zeal for the unity of the Body of Christ.' The report of the 10th Assembly of the Conference of European Churches held in Prague (1-11 September 1992) contains this comment: 'Living together with differences means to be called to mutual respect and acceptance, and unity is not the end of diversity but of division.'

Ecumenism is not just an optional extra to be indulged in by a select few. It goes to the very heart of the gospel message. It is inherent in the unity of the Blessed Trinity – three Persons and one God. It is implicit when we claim to be 'in Christ', because to be 'in Christ' is to have an identity that overrides all other identities. This points to the danger of over emphasising individual church identity, and that is something we can all do at times. The way one modern theologian, Frances Young, has put it is this: 'Controversy should not be a vehicle for conceit, competition and envy,' and she goes on, 'It is things which matter for our identity which trigger human pride and jealousy. The new identity in Christ should mean that such passions are transcended.'

The ecumenical nature of the gospel message is one with which many feel uncomfortable today, and that for a variety of reasons, ranging from fear of absorption to dilution of fundamentals. Yet to deny this criterion of authenticity is to risk withdrawal into a denominational and, what is even worse, a judgmental cocoon, and to deny the reality of our Lord's own prayer 'that they may all be one ... so that world may believe...'

And so the church's message to be worthwhile must be God-centred, experiential, relevant, compassionate and ecumenical. If it is, then, according to the words in Jeremiah, there is a two fold promise: 'You will be my prophet again' and 'the people will come back to you.'

These two thoughts are not without significance as we begin our deliberations in Synod. The prophetic voice – how often has the church been challenged to fill that role? May what is said and done during the coming days enable the Church of Ireland to be seen in that capacity. If that is what happens then there will surely be a response on the part of the people. And they will come back, not just in a bare statistical sense under a census heading, but they will come back in heart and mind to the God revealed in Jesus Christ, and in coming back will herald a fresh era of hope for the church and for society.

CHAPTER 20

Ezekiel Chapter 1 Verse 3:
'The word of the Lord came to Ezekiel the priest,
the Son of Buzi, in the land of the Chaldeans by the river
Chebar; and the hand of the Lord was upon him there.'

Travel if you will back some two and a half thousand years in time. Picture a settlement of refugees by a river. They longed for their homeland, and that longing was expressed by the psalmist in words that have passed into popular usage: 'By the waters of Babylon, there we sat down and wept, when we remembered Zion' (Ps 137:1).

It was a period of deep depression for the refugees or exiles, who longed for their homeland and in particular for the worship of the temple at Jerusalem. But those in the homeland were going their own way, oblivious to all moral or spiritual restraints. Indeed the way things were going it was likely that the country would be overrun again and further ravaged.

However, among the refugees was one man of vision who tried to speak to the situation. Even at a distance of some seven hundred miles he tried to warn the people of the folly of their ways, and in those days the communications gap would not have been easily bridged.

The results of this man's efforts have left us with one of the most outstanding books in the bible, the Book of the Prophet Ezekiel. It has been well said that even among those very great men, the Hebrew prophets, Ezekiel was great. Apart from his courage and moral strength there is a contemporary ring about the book which enables those of every generation to learn from it something of the nature of God's dealings with his people.

The first lesson is that God chooses spokespersons for himself, and sometimes these are the most unlikely people from the most unlikely places.

Ezekiel was a refugee and he spent most of his days as a priest ministering to a few people in an obscure corner of

Babylon, but he was chosen by God to bring a message of hope and renewal. He was a reluctant spokesman, just as Moses had been a reluctant leader before him. But the hand of God was upon him and he responded.

Having responded, Ezekiel was encouraged not to be afraid. He was enabled. 'And when he spoke to me, the Spirit entered into me and set me upon my feet' (2:2). As we look out on the whole panoramic view of God's activity in history, we cannot but be struck by the fact that God uses on occasions the most unlikely people to further his cause. The bible is full of such people – the slave boy Joseph, the herdsman Moses, the shepherd lad David, the earthy fisherman Peter, the anti-Christian fanatic Paul. Although from different backgrounds they all have one thing in common, they were empowered for the work to which they had been called. Using Ezekiel's own imagery of the valley of dry bones (37), no matter how lifeless the bones are, once they have been infused with the Spirit they can live and stand upon their feet. It is a stirring thought and one which should fill with confidence all those who respond to the call of God.

But Ezekiel was encouraged and empowered for a particular reason which lies at the heart of the matter. His commission was 'you shall speak my words to them, whether they hear or refuse to hear.' God requires those whom he has called to speak his words. 'Thus says the Lord' was the great theme of the Old Testament prophets. It is a phrase which we need to rediscover in our own day. To rediscover not just the phrase itself but the implications of it. There are many ready and willing to harangue others with their views and advice, but rarely do we catch an echo of 'thus says the Lord.' It was only when Ezekiel could speak in that vein that the people would recognise that there had been a prophet among them (2:5).

How does the prophet in any generation arrive at the point of saying with confidence 'thus says the Lord?' How does he achieve recognition? How does he come to be accepted as proclaiming an authentic word and not a counterfeit? Religion has its share of spurious leaders.

Ezekiel describes this in vivid symbolic terms. 'And he said to me, "Son of man, eat what is offered to you; eat this scroll, and go, speak to the house of Israel".' The scroll is symbolic of the spiritual nourishment which is necessary if the prophet is to speak the authentic and authoritative message of God. Even in a computerised age this principle is still true. The message of God can only be relayed in so far as it it has been imbibed in the first place. No one can hope to be an authentic messenger of God, interpreting the will of God, who has not been nourished and sustained by the food of God, and the food of God is basically that supplied by the church of God – worship, sacraments, prayer, bible.

Today we hear much talk about a crisis of leadership. Have we not a right to ask of our leaders, not just Church leaders, but any who would seek to influence others, what is the scroll on which you are being fed? What is it that motivates and sustains you and determines the message you are proclaiming? If it is composed of such elements as mere tradition, expediency and self-interest, then the prophetic voice will be weak and leadership will rest with those described by Ezekiel as unfaithful shepherds. But if the scroll has a spiritual content then people will indeed know that there are prophets in their midst.

CHAPTER 21

Daniel Chapter 9 Verse 6:
'We have not listened to thy servants the prophets,
who spoke in thy name, to our kings, our princes,
and our fathers, and to all the people of the land.'

Which book in the bible is most frequently used as a source for sermon texts? Certainly not the Book of Daniel if I am to judge from my own experience of three texts in over forty years. Just as many people tend to be selective in their bible reading so too most preachers tend to be selective in their choice of biblical material on which to base their few well chosen words week by week. Often the Old Testament is neglected and we fail to treat the bible as a unit.

True, our Christian faith centres on a person, Jesus Christ, and on an event, the Cross, but the Old Testament not only points forward to these and prepares us for them, it also teaches us lessons that are of fundamental importance, lessons concerning the sovereignty of God and the purposes of God in the lives of individuals and nations. In its pages we have a panoramic view of God in action, God working his purpose out. But above all else, we have a graphic picture of what happens when the voice of God is shut out and the commandments of God are broken.

Take, for example, the words from Daniel 9:6. Experts may differ over who wrote them or when they were written, but it is patently obvious that the writer is saying something very definite about the misfortunes of the Children of Israel, their exile and their persecution. Basically the point being made is that they have been brought about by a refusal to listen to the prophets who were the religious leaders of the day. The prophets interpreted the will of God for the people, but their voice had been neglected with disastrous consequences.

Furthermore the morality of the people had sunk to a low ebb. Their moral backbone had been weakened by a life com-

pletely out of touch with the voice of prophecy and out of conformity with the commandments of God. As a result, the fibre of
national life could not withstand the attacks from outside nations.
The Children of Israel were wide open, not just militarily, but
morally and spiritually, to attack and ultimate defeat.

One aspect of the bible sometimes forgotten is that it is a
book for all times. When we delve into the Old Testament we are
not just reading a stirring historical saga of one nation, we are in
fact seeing unfolding before us the dealings of God with humanity. And because God is not a fickle God of whims and caprice,
the lessons we learn are timeless and ever relevant.

It is this thought that encourages us today to turn afresh to a
verse like that from Daniel and re-read it in the light of contemporary society.

CHAPTER 22

Hosea Chapter 11 Verse 8:
'How can I give you up, O Ephraim?
How can I hand you over, O Israel.'

Few words in the Old Testament, indeed few words in the bible, are more poignant than these from the Book of Hosea.

Hosea preached in the Northern Kingdom of Israel in troubled times before its fall. He was especially concerned about the idolatry of the people and their faithlessness towards God. He graphically pictured this in terms of his own disastrous marriage to an unfaithful woman, Gomer, a prostitute. Just as she was unfaithful to her husband, so God's people had deserted their Lord, and for this they would be judged.

Yet in the end, Hosea was convinced that God's constant and unswerving love for his people would prevail and he would win back the nation to himself and restore the severed relationship. Few books in the Old Testament point forward more graphically to the New Testament and the supreme act of love revealed by God in Jesus Christ on the Cross. True love is distinguished by its ability to go on loving even when the object of that love has become unlovable. As it was with Hosea and his faithless wife, so it is with God. He goes on loving us and longing for our response.

The twin concepts of faithlessness and forgiveness, so vividly illustrated in the Book of Hosea, are at the heart of the Christian gospel. Indeed the very word 'gospel', good news, reminds us of this fact. Once we begin to move away from the central theme of Christianity and consign the central figure to the wings then we begin to develop caricatures of Christianity and peripheral concerns begin to dominate. Faithlessness may even take on the mantle of a crusade. In a TV discussion a few years ago on the role of the missionary today there was much talk about imposing an alien culture on people in Africa and South America. There was trenchant criticism of the disturbing effect this has on people whose traditions go back for centuries. It was argued that it is better to leave such people alone. Through all the discussion it was difficult to discern any real appreciation of the central tenet of Christianity, that it has less to do with culture and much more to do with the inner freedom that comes with the acceptance of forgiveness. Christianity does not deny to people their cultural inheritance, rather it seeks to commend 'the more excellent way', a way which does not necessarily lead to political freedom or an abundance of this world's goods, but rather to the paradox expressed by St Paul 'as having nothing and yet possessing all things.'

But faithlessness is not just a personal characteristic. In the Book of Hosea, although the illustration is couched in terms of a relationship between two individuals, the real faithless party is the nation – 'return, O Israel, to the Lord your God.'

This leads to the searching question, how far have we as a nation been faithful to our Christian heritage or do we stand accused of faithlessness?

That we have a Christian heritage we must never forget. When we speak of the island of saints and scholars we are speaking of a reality to which Slane, Tara, Downpatrick, the Book of Kells, the Book of Durrow and the chalice of Derrynaflan give substance. Have we been faithful to this heritage, or have we pandered to what A. M. Allchin has described as 'the pretensions of the twentieth century?'

But here we must be careful and not fall into the trap of equating our heritage completely with what can be seen, touched and handled. In the long run these treasures speak to us of a deeper heritage, the heritage of faith.

We look then to our country in terms of its spirituality. As a country to which the name of Christian is still applied, what is the reading on the spiritual barometer? How far are the Christian virtues and values in evidence?

By and large it is a barren scene, with aggression and a lack of regard for people and property writ large on the face of society. Here and there we find oases in the desert, such as the response to Third World tragedies and the work of voluntary organis-ations. But if we look at the broad canvas of national life, can we be really happy that the country merits the name Christian?

At such times there is a natural tendency to despair. Yet it is at such times that the Christian can bring his faith to bear on the situation in the knowledge that this is God's world which can only achieve its deepest fulfilment and satisfaction and freedom when the Lord of Lords and King of Kings is given his rightful place. The life of Jesus Christ shows what is involved in this: friendship of the sinner, feeding the hungry, caring for the out-cast.

It is at this point that the words from Hosea speak to our situation, reminding us that God's mercy and love and forgiveness are such that he, from the depths of his being, longs for our response and will not fail us when it is given – 'How can I give you up, O Ephraim, how can I hand you over, O Israel?'

CHAPTER 23

Amos Chapter 7 Verse 7:
'Behold, the Lord was standing beside a wall
built with a plumb line.'

The church is not in the business of party politics, certainly not the Church of Ireland. But occasionally we all need to be reminded of our duty to vote. It is a privilege accorded in a free society. To neglect it is to neglect one of the great responsibilities laid upon us as citizens. Bearing in mind Our Lord's attitude to the civil authorities, it is in fact a Christian duty. How we vote is our personal decision, but that we do vote, having weighed up the relevant issues, is of fundamental importance.

Now it may seem a far cry from an Old Testament book dating from the eighth century B.C. to contemporary society, yet because the Word of God is living and active, speaking to every generation, we do well to ponder what was said by the prophet Amos.

Amos was a forthright prophet, called by God to deliver a message to the leaders of Israel at a time when society was fast becoming more and more corrupt. It was a deceptive situation. There was no slackening of religious observance, indeed quite the contrary. The country was not at war, in fact it was enjoying a period of comparative tranquillity and prosperity.

However it was this very atmosphere of affluence that led to what are sometimes described as 'the sins of peace'. 'Woe to them that are at ease in Zion' thunders the prophet as he castigates society and condemns the social and economic injustice, the dishonesty and sexual vice that were flourishing.

His method was through the interpretation of a series of visions, one of which was that of a plumb line.

'He showed me: behold, the Lord was standing beside a wall built with a plumb line, with a plumb line in his hand ... Then the Lord said, "Behold, I am setting a plumb line in the midst of my people Israel; I will never again pass by them".'

In building, a plumb line is used as a guide to make sure that walls are straight and that the whole building is in order and will stand firmly and squarely. According to Amos the same is true for society. There must be a moral plumb line, there must be guidelines which we can use to ensure that the building, the structure of society, will stand securely.

Looking at the Book of Amos as a whole, these guidelines revolve around our understanding of God and his relationship with the world.

The first guideline is that God is a God of the whole earth. As such his rule extends to all aspects of life, including our communal and commercial relationships. It was neglect of this fact that was leading the Israelites down the slippery slope of corruption. True, they kept up their religious observance, but in a mechanical way. Outside the formal religious context anything went – dishonest dealing, overcharging and falsifying weights.

Complementing that message was his proclamation of a God whose character was absolutely righteous, and as a result demanded righteousness from his people. To carry a sense of righteousness into the whole of life, that was the vocation of Amos, what he believed he was called to do by God.

It is this aspect of Amos that makes the book so contemporary. His message was unpalatable and unpopular, but it was needed to bring people back to a worthwhile way of life.

Who is to say that the same does not apply today? How far is righteousness, within which is summed up such concepts as truth, honesty and purity, the standard by which modern society lives? The signs are all around us that where righteousness is flouted, society as a whole and individuals within society, suffer.

Amos sought to restore the spiritual backbone to Israel. Without that backbone the nation was sinking faster and faster into the slough of despond. He realised that there had to be a standard other than that of self-interest and he found this in the righteousness of the God of the whole earth. We do well to reflect on his words.

CHAPTER 24

Micah Chapter 6 Verses 7 and 8:
'Will the Lord be pleased with thousands of rams,
with ten thousands of rivers of oil? ...
He has showed you, O man, what is good;
and what does the Lord require of you but to do justice,
and to love kindness, and to walk humbly with your God.'

Even a casual reader of the bible will realise that in turning from the Old Testament to the New Testament one is moving from one atmosphere to another. Generally speaking there is a harshness about the Old not found in the New Testament, an emphasis on the law and specific regulations.

But here and there the voice of a prophet breaks through modifying the harshness of the atmosphere. Such a one was Micah. What a wonderful picture of peace he gives in the fourth chapter – 'they shall beat their swords into ploughshares, and their spears into pruning hooks.'

However, it is later on in chapter six that we have the text for which he is best remembered, words which have been described as one of the greatest passages in all religious literature, 'He has showed you, O man, what is good; and what does the Lord require of you but to do justice, and to love kindness, and to walk humbly with your God.'

Like other Old Testament words, in order to appreciate them fully we need to understand the circumstances in which they were written.

Micah prophesied in the Southern Kingdom of Judah. The situation prevailing was well fitted to call forth the fiery indignation of one of God's prophets. Oppression was rife, and the rich landowners, supported by unjust judges, saw to it that the poor had no redress. The priests were also on the side of the wealthy, while many a prophet could be found to flatter those in power in order to secure his own position.

Alongside this corruption was a type of religion which

thought that God's favour could be bought. Give a wealthy offering of rams or oil and that would keep him pleased. Such was
the sterile mentality of the day.

But then along came Micah cutting through the pretence.
'Will the Lord be pleased with thousands of rams, with ten thou-
sands of rivers of oil?' Such was the relevant question posed by
Micah, and back came the direct reply pointing out that what
God required above all else was for people 'to do justice, and to
love kindness, and to walk humbly with your God.'

When we consider the state of the country we can begin to
realise just how revolutionary this answer really was. Justice
was non existent, mercy and kindness were unheard of, humility
before God was not something to be prized. But the voice of
God, speaking through his prophets, proclaimed justice, mercy
and humility as the cornerstone for those who wished to do the
will of God.

What makes this passage so outstanding is that it foreshadows
the character which Our Lord in the New Testament urges his
followers to cultivate, it foreshadows the revelation of God in
Jesus Christ. In Christ we see justice, mercy and humility per-
sonified. The words of Micah came to life in Bethlehem and
walked the countryside of Palestine, urging those with whom he
came in contact to follow him.

Viewed in this light we see just how deep was the insight of
the Old Testament prophet when he uttered the words that have
inspired men and women down the centuries and set a standard
for society based on justice, mercy and humility.

CHAPTER 25

Zephaniah Chapter 3 Verse 14:
'Sing aloud, O daughter of Zion; shout, O Israel!
Rejoice and exult with all your heart, O daughter of Jerusalem.'

Search the scriptures and it would be difficult to find words of a more joyful character than these from Zephaniah. They come from a little known and seldom read book, and are thought to have been written during the period of the great exile of the Children of Israel in Babylon.

The morale of the people was low, the outlook for the future was bleak, freedom was limited. They were strangers in a strange land, set in the midst of an alien people. Their thoughts must have turned to their homeland and in particular to Jerusalem and the temple. This attitude of mind was summed up so well by the psalmist when he wrote the poignant words, 'By the waters of Babylon there we sat down and wept, when we remembered Zion.'

In this situation it was necessary to keep the flame of hope burning even if it flickered fitfully at times.

But during the exile there were some who could look beyond the present difficulties, people of vision whose faith in God gave them this confident hope in the future, leaders who transmitted their optimism to those around them, and did it in language such as that found in Zephaniah:

The Lord, your God, is in your midst,
A warrior who gives victory;
He will rejoice over you with gladness,
He will renew you in his love;
He will exult over you with loud singing
As on a day of festival. (3:17)

The Book of Zephaniah would hardly come in the top ten of the biblical charts, but the message it conveys is an appropriate one for those who live in the post-resurrection era where hope, confidence and optimism should be paramount, and where joy should be an integral part of life. 'Sing', 'shout', 'rejoice', are words that should be part of the Christian vocabulary, even more so than in Old Testament times.

Certainly in the early church this message of joy was spelled out in large letters as typified by St Paul when he encouraged his converts to 'rejoice evermore'. All the evidence points to a community that gave vent to its joy and deep-seated happiness, not least in the singing of hymns. It is not without significance that some centuries later the followers of St Francis of Assissi were known as 'God's Jesters' because of their joyful demeanour, while the poet Rabelais summed up the matter so well when he said:

One inch of joy surmounts of grief a span,

Because to laugh is proper to the man.

But the joy of which the bible speaks must not be confused with superficiality. Rather it springs from a deep-rooted confidence and serenity based, not only on faith in God's purposes as typified by the words of Zephaniah to the exiles in Babylon, but also on the fact of the resurrection through which, as Peter reminds us, we have been 'born anew to a living hope'. It is because of that hope that we can take the Old Testament words and reincarnate them in a Christian context and rejoice and exult with all our heart.

CHAPTER 26

Zechariah Chapter 8 Verse 23:
'Let us go with you, for we have heard that God is with you.'

Zechariah had a vision; a vision of Jerusalem restored and the temple rebuilt. He had a vision of people from many nations coming to Jerusalem to worship the Lord Almighty. He had a vision of ten foreigners coming to one Jew and saying, 'Let us go with you for we have heard that God is with you', or as it is expressed in the Good News Bible, 'we want to share your destiny, because we have heard that God is with you.'

These words contain a vision of hope and joyful expectation. But they also pose a challenge. Basically they have to do with example or impression, of people relating to people because of something that touches their innermost being.

'Let us go with you', 'let us share your destiny', said those foreigners, not because you are Jews, not because of your temple, not because you have cheated the odds and survived, but let us go with you for 'we have heard that God is with you'.

What do those words mean in the various contexts of Church life?

(1) First, as individuals and members of this Diocesan Synod. Do they not challenge us to reflect on our way of life and whether it is God-centred in terms of such matters as truth, honesty and behaviour? It will be difficult for us to spend our time together today in an honest searching after the will of God unless we are prepared to acknowledge the rule of God in our lives as individuals. If we so acknowledge God then we can indeed differ in our views, but the manner of our differing will be such that at the end of the day people will still be able to say, 'Let us go with you, for we have heard that God is with you'.

(2) In Synod we meet also as representatives of the various parishes in the diocese. Here too the words of Zechariah challenge us, and challenge us in a very searching way. Could peo-

ple looking at our parishes in terms of attitude and worship be compelled to say 'let us go with you for we have heard that God is with you', the God revealed in Jesus Christ and characterised by such marks as reconciliation and forgiveness?

(3) But we meet, not just as representatives from a variety of parishes, we meet as a body to do the business of the diocese. What then is the view we form of the diocese as a whole in the context of Zechariah's words? What in other words are the signs of the Kingdom in our midst? Let me mention four. First, there is the variety of people at various stages in their vocational search and training for the ministry. In the second place, there is the outstanding group of laity who are prepared to serve the diocese in so many ways. Thirdly, there is the level of giving for relief and development, in particular through the Bishops' Appeal. And fourthly, there is the faithful pastoral ministry of our parochial clergy who in many cases work in isolation and cover vast areas.

All of this and much more prompts me to say that people could look at us and our expectation might well be summed up in Zechariah's words. This is not to be complacent. There are many problems in our midst, but it is to recognise some of the positive elements with which we are blessed.

We meet then as individuals, as parochial representatives and as part of a diocese. But we meet also within the total framework of the Church of Ireland, at a time when our minority voice has a real contribution to make to Irish society. Apart from agendas altogether, the way we do our business is being scrutinised closely. The rational, balanced approach to problems, coupled with the transparency and accountability that characterises our deliberations, commends itself to many people. This too in its own way is a sign that God is with us, and we must guard these elements of our life lest they be swallowed up by the expediency of modern society. In the end what we say will be of less importance than what we are, and this is borne out by a modern writer, Raymond Fung. He speaks of a growing inclination for people to inch their way back to the Christian Faith. In this process, he says, they are whispering some of the deepest questions to us. 'Do you know God?' And he goes on, 'If they sense that we do not, because of our busyness or because we haven't really listened to their question, then they will go away again, perhaps this time more sadly than cynically. And if they sense that we do, it will not be because we say we do. It will be because they see it in the way we live.'

CHAPTER 27

Malachi Chapter 3 Verse 1:
'The Lord whom you seek will suddenly come to his temple.'

Perhaps we are more familiar with the beginning of this verse from the final book of the Old Testament – 'Behold I send my messenger to prepare the way before me.' We know that these words found fulfilment in John the Baptist.

The words following, 'the Lord whom you seek will suddenly come to his temple', also foretell a coming event, and when Our Lord came to earth they too were literally fulfilled in the story of the presentation of Christ in the temple as recorded in Luke (2:22-24).

What took place dated back to the old Mosaic law (Ex 13:1-2). According to this, every firstborn son should be holy to the Lord, to attend the service of the temple or tabernacle, or else be redeemed with an offering of money or sacrifice.

But as well as this presentation of the child, the mother also had a duty to perform. She was obliged to separate herself from the congregation for forty days after the birth of a male and eighty after the birth of a female, and then if in good circumstances she was to present a lamb, but if poor a couple of pigeons. All these legal requirements were performed after the birth of Our Lord.

When we consider this childhood story of Christ in the temple, and when we further consider the obedience which later he was to give to the rules and customs of religion, we are reminded that behind the obedience there was deep humility of spirit. Willing obedience always calls for a measure of humility, unless it is motivated by fear, and then it is no longer real obedience but coercion.

The humility of Our Lord as the pattern for Christian character, that is the thought implicit in the temple incident.

Think of Our Lord as the sinless one. Surely he was under no obligation to obey the religious laws of his day, which were later described graphically by Paul in the Authorised Version as a schoolmaster. Yet he obeyed. It is but an example of that humility which Paul exhorts the Philippines to display when he says 'Let this mind be in you which was also in Christ Jesus.' And not only humbling himself to be made in human likeness, but being born into a humble working home. This is emphasised in that there is no mention of the offering of a lamb which would have signified wealthy parentage, but only of a pair of turtledoves or two young pigeons which were offered by those of limited means.

This beginning was in keeping with what was to follow all through Our Lord's life, the thread of humility, which so often contrasts with the ideas of the world.

What are some of the phrases in common currency? 'Getting on in the world'; 'Climbing the ladder'; 'Keeping ahead in the race.' So often getting on, and climbing, and keeping ahead, are achieved at the expense of somebody else. It is here that the church is faced with one of its major tasks, that of seeing how the principles it preaches can be applied to the life of the individual and to a complex society. One of the principles high on the list is humility.

This task is no new one. It is as old as Christianity itself, and is made no easier when the church is guilty of a lack of humility in its own life. How much disunity exists in the church today because of this? Honour and dignity must be satisfied. The initial major break between Christians, the break between East and West, symbolised by Patriarch and Pope, was largely due to Constantinople and Rome climbing on the pedestal of dignity.

If the Christian is to be recognised as authentic, then humility must be a constant and recurring feature of life. Not like the lady of whom Henry James wrote, 'at moments she discovered she was grotesquely wrong, and then she treated herself to a week of passionate humility.'

The message of our Lord's presentation in the Temple, with all its Old Testament overtones reflecting the words from Malachi, is a message of obedience and humility. This act performed by his parents in obedience to the law was but the prelude to a life of humble service which set the pattern for his followers in all ages.

CHAPTER 28

Matthew Chapter 11 Verse 15:
'He who has ears to hear let him hear.'

One of the unobtrusive organisations within the Church of Ireland is the Adult Mission to the Deaf and Dumb. Through its work many who might otherwise feel isolated from the life of the church are enabled to be a part of its fellowship. Each year when, in the gospel reading, we recall Our Lord's healing of the deaf and dumb man, the work of this particular Mission is prayerfully upheld.

But deafness is not just physical. There is also spiritual deafness, not so obvious but nonetheless real. It could be described as our failure to hear the voice of God.

It is this ability to hear and respond to the voice of God that characterises great religious leaders. They have spiritual alertness or sensitivity.

In the Old Testament this typified the great prophets. 'Thus says the Lord' was their constant theme. Because they were attuned to God they could interpret his will to their fellow men and women at a particular time, and so be regarded as God's spokesmen.

In the New Testament a recurring phrase in Our Lord's teaching was 'He who has ears to hear let him hear.' Our Lord knew that many of those who were listening to him with their outward ears were deaf in their inward ears, and so his message made no real impact on them.

This has always been a present reality. 'Where are the prophets today?' is a question frequently heard in church circles. In other words, where are those who are recognised as proclaiming the will of God because they are living close to God?

Whether or not spiritual deafness is more prevalent today than at other times is open to debate, but one thing is certain, there are circumstances today which make it difficult to hear the voice of God.

Two in particular:

(1) In the first place we are conditioned by a scientific outlook on life which seeks to limit all experiences to those of the senses, so that only what can be seen and touched is regarded as real.

Some years ago a well-known Church of Ireland clergyman, Archdeacon Giff, himself a scientist, wrote on his subject: 'By means of our whole praying and worshipping actions we receive God's signals, and we learn to interpret them. Or rather, we can learn, if we have a desire to do so, if we are prepared to experiment for ourselves and to take the help of those who have been masters of devotion.' He went on to give a fascinating illustration from George Bernard Shaw's play *St Joan:* 'The Dauphin contends that he never hears the voices which Joan claims are guiding her. "They come to you," she replies, "but you do not listen. You have not sat in the field in the evening and considered their message. When the Angelus rings you cross yourself, and are done with it; but if you prayed from your heart and listened to the thrilling of the bells in the air, after they stopped ringing you would hear the same voices as I do".'

(2) In the second place, achieving spiritual awareness is hindered by something which affects us all: the pace of life.

Spiritual perception or insight is not achieved overnight. It is not an instant commodity that comes pre-packed. It requires perseverance and training – in a word, time. The professional, the tradesman, and the farmer do not become experts overnight. They must spend time, often a great deal of time, and even when qualified they go on learning. So too in our understanding and experience of the spiritual, we must spend time in growth.

Many years ago I spent two weeks of the summer in a college in Canterbury. Along with others I became involved in helping to conduct the thousands of visitors around the cathedral. At the end of the two weeks the great building was beginning to speak to me and reveal something of its inner message. But it took time, and I doubt if those who paid a fleeting visit before proceeding to the next guidebook attraction heard very much in the depths of their being.

In the bible a small but significant word is 'wait'. 'They who wait for the Lord shall renew their strength' (Is 40:31). The thought is transferred into one of our well known hymns: 'Speak Lord in the stillness, while I wait on thee.'

We must give time if we want to deepen our spiritual alertness, to save ourselves from spiritual deafness, and develop again the hearing ear.

Matthew Chapter 18 Verses 34 and 35:
'And in anger his lord delivered him to the jailers,
till he should pay all his debt.
So also my heavenly Father will do to every one of you,
if you do not forgive your brother from your heart.'

Some years ago a former Archbishop of Capetown, the late Joost de Blank, wrote a very telling little book entitled *The Uncomfortable Words*. As the title suggests, the archbishop expounded some of the sayings of Jesus which were in contrast to those used in the Holy Communion service, and which we have come to know as the comfortable words because of the assurance they give when we hear them; for example, 'Come to me, all that labour and are heavy laden, and I will refresh you' (Mt 11:28).

It is of course important that we should have this assurance of God's mercy and forgiveness firmly grounded in our hearts. It is the very core of our faith, its unique ingredient. But here and there throughout Our Lord's ministry he inserts something of a harsher note. It was as though he wanted his listeners to stop and think for a moment lest they become too self-satisfied and self-indulgent, too much at ease in Zion. And so we have these uncomfortable words cropping up from time to time which must be taken into account in any analysis of the total gospel.

One such uncomfortable word is found in Matthew in the parable of the unforgiving servant. It tells of a servant who, having been forgiven a large debt by his master, refuses in turn to forgive a fellow servant a much smaller debt, whereupon his master casts him into prison until he has paid all.

This parable is found only in Matthew. However, it is not to be regarded as an isolated instance of Our Lord's reference to forgiveness. This is a theme which keeps coming to the fore all through his teaching. It is emphasised in The Lord's Prayer, stressed in the parable of the Prodigal Son, and highlighted in the

word from the Cross, 'Father forgive them,' to give but a few obvious examples.

Our Lord's teaching on forgiveness in the present context follows from Peter's question, 'How often shall my brother sin
against me, and I forgive him?' (Mt 18:21). His personal opinion
was that seven times would be sufficient. This was a sacred number and a favourite in the bible, and so there was some significance in Peter's suggestion. Furthermore, the Jewish masters
taught their followers to forgive three times, and so seven was
quite a liberal advance.

But the whole point of the parable is to illustrate that we must
not reckon forgiveness in a mechanical manner. It is not a commodity to be put into a compartment and brought out for use when con-
venient. Rather is should be a part of our make-up as Christians.
This is what Our Lord was underlining when he spoke of forgiving
'from your hearts'. It should be treated as an attitude rather than an
act. It is what has been described as an active process.

It is at this point in the parable that we come to the uncomfortable word. The unmerciful servant, having been forgiven his
great debt, would not in turn forgive his fellow servant a small
debt. And so we read, 'in anger his lord delivered him to the jailers, till be should pay all his debt.' Then the warning is made personal, 'So also my heavenly Father will do to every one of you, if
you do not forgive your brother from your heart.'

While this is indeed an uncomfortable word it does focus our
minds on the concept of forgiveness. In doing that, at least three
comments can be made.

The first is that forgiveness is at the heart of the Christian
gospel. 'Christianity', said H. R. Mackintosh, 'overcame by means
of its message of forgiveness, in which it had no rival.' And he
goes on to say, 'Among the possible brief phrases in which the
essence of Christianity might fairly be summed up, one certainly
would be, I believe in God who forgives sins, through Jesus
Christ.' Which is really another way of saying, as the Creed does,
'I believe ... in the forgiveness of sins.'

Again, C. S. Lewis in his classic little book, *Mere Christianity*,
has a section on forgiveness which he describes as the most un-

popular Christian virtue, because our reception of God's forgiveness depends on our willingness to forgive others.

This leads on to the second point which is that it is a mistake
for us to imagine that we can be in a right relationship with God
so long as we are maintaining a wrong attitude towards our fellow men and women. Over and over again, the bible points to this
interaction between God and neighbour, expressed in its most
familiar form in The Lord's Prayer – 'Forgive us our sins as we
forgive those who sin against us.' In other words, if we fail to forgive can we expect God to forgive us?

The third point arises out of this. Forgiveness is not always
easy to exercise. It can be misconstrued and interpreted as a sign
of weakness. Yet despite this we must persist because it is the will
of God as revealed in Jesus Christ, and when we do persist we invariably find that we are upheld by the grace of God.

Those clergy who were in the midst of the turmoil in Northern
Ireland tell of the remarkable capacity for forgiveness on the part
of many who, at first sight, appeared to have most cause for bitter-
ness. Yet often the cry for revenge came from those not directly affected by tragedy, while those most directly affected were most
ready to forgive. Indeed, it may well be that when history comes
to evaluate the church's role in the twenty-five year tragedy of
Northern Ireland this capacity to forgive will be seen in its true
light as a major contribution to stability in a situation where civil
war was forecast more than once.

The issues raised by this familiar parable of the unforgiving
servant are weighty and personal. We are told unmistakably that
forgiveness is not to be treated in terms of arithmetic, with a special limit attached to the seven times tables. Rather it must be seen
as an integral part of the Christian's lifestyle which conditions
entrance to the kingdom of heaven.

Expressed in the words of the New English Bible we are left in
no doubt. 'And so angry was the master that he condemned the
man to torture until he should pay the debt in full. And that is
how my heavenly Father will deal with you, unless you each forgive your brother from your hearts.' Truly an uncomfortable
word.

CHAPTER 30

Matthew Chapter 8 Verse 34:
'And when they saw him
they begged him to leave their neighbourhood.'

Few passages in the bible make sadder reading than these words from Matthew. They come as the climax to a very dramatic incident where two people possessed by devils are exorcised by Jesus. The devils then entered into a herd of swine, who in turn rushed headlong into the sea and were drowned.

One can imagine the keepers of the herd taking flight and dashing back into the city and the inhabitants, perhaps out of curiosity, hurrying out to the scene of the incident. There they beg Jesus to leave their neighbourhood.

On at least one other occasion Jesus had been asked to depart. The disciples had been fishing and, having toiled all night, had caught nothing. At the command of Jesus they had cast their nets again into the water and caught a great shoal of fish. When Peter saw what had happened his response was, 'Depart from me for I am a sinful man, O Lord.' Here the request was bound up with the feeling of unworthiness to be in the presence of Jesus, an attitude which must always be present before we can make progress in our spiritual pilgrimage. The familiar words of the hymn sum it up: 'I am not worthy, holy Lord, that thou shouldst come to me.'

However, in the incident in Matthew there is no such expression of unworthiness on the part of the crowd. If anything it is concern at the material loss occasioned by the flight and destruction of the herd of swine. Possibly they were quite content to have the two possessed with devils in their midst. In many parts of Ireland, especially in rural areas, there is an 'odd' character who is part and parcel of the local scene. But when Christ comes he cannot acquiesce in anything that is imperfect. So the devils were cast out with dramatic effect, and the people begged him to leave the area.

This request is more common that we may imagine. Think of it in terms of society today and ask, is Christ present or have we banished him?

There is a tendency today to think of Christianity in individualistic terms. This may well reflect the world in which we live where so often the individual is glorified, be it pop star or sporting idol. It is highlighted in the religious sense by the appeal of the mass evangelists whose so-called charisma can even exude from the television screen.

It is of course right and proper that faith should make a personal appeal, a personal demand for commitment, as for example at Confirmation. Without this, Christianity can have no real root in the hearts and minds of people. But it must also be seen in a broader context if it is to be truly relevant. It must be seen as permeating society at large, not just in a series of laws and regulations, but in attitudes and actions.

Does the society of which we are a part, and which we help to mould, reflect the mind of Christ? Or are we among those who have besought Christ to depart out of our coasts? Can we square so much that is happening today with the presence of Christ – murder, vandalism, disregard for truth, exploitation of human weakness through drugs, sexual permissiveness and child abuse? So much that is happening gives credence to the phrase, 'A Godless society,' a society that has banished Christ from its shores.

Yet there are many who would claim that we are a Christian country, and point to the fact that we have more clergy per head of the population than most other countries, while there are comparatively few people who would not be listed under the heading of some Christian tradition.   Could it be that if we have not besought Christ to depart out of our coasts we are ignoring his presence, reluctant to face up to the demands he makes. That famous padre of the first world war, Studdart Kennedy, 'Woodbine Willie', put it graphically in one of his many poems:

'When Jesus came to Birmingham
They simply passed Him bye
They didn't touch a hair of Him
They simply let Him die.'

Either way then, whether we have besought Christ to depart or are simply ignoring him, we have much heartsearching to do as a society. And this is true at every level, church and state, media and professions, especially those who influence the young. The list is endless because we are all a part of society and are caught up in the tide of events.

Our prayer could well be in the familiar words of the baptismal service, 'that we may never be ashamed to confess the faith of Christ crucified but manfully to fight under his banner against sin, the world and the devil, and so continue Christ's faithful soldier and servant unto our lives end.'

CHAPTER 31

Matthew Chapter 12 Verse 42:
'Something greater than Solomon is here.'

'The wisdom of Solomon', like 'the patience of Job', is one of those phrases which has found its way into our everyday form of speech. It is based on the famous incident in the Old Testament where Solomon, having chosen the gift of under-standing from God, used it to decide which of two women was the rightful mother of a young child.

The words from Matthew 12 refer back to another famous event in the Old Testament, the visit of the Queen of Sheba to the court of King Solomon.

Solomon's reputation had spread far and wide, and the Queen had come to see for herself the magnificence of the court and the grandeur of the temple. She had also come to listen to Solomon's wisdom, the type of homespun wisdom found in the Book of Proverbs, to which Solomon's name is ascribed.

Taking all these factors together Solomon has acquired an aura of greatness. Yet in Matthew, Our Lord indicates that 'something greater than Solomon is here' – that he himself was greater than Solomon.

In what sense was Our Lord greater than Solomon? Certainly not in terms of earthy possessions or worldly goods. One of the reasons why the Queen of Sheba came to visit Solomon was because she had heard of the splendour of his court, his riches, the number of his servants and the type of regal authority he exercised over his subjects. Her famous comment when she had seen it all was 'behold, half was not told me.'

Contrast that picture with the life of the Son of Man – 'Foxes have holes and birds of the air have nests; but the Son of Man has nowhere to lay his head.' Whatever greatness meant in Our Lord's eyes it had little to do with material possessions, with what is so often regarded as greatness in the eyes of the world.

Wherein then did Our Lord's greatness lie? We can look for

an answer to that question in at least three directions, summed up in three words; Purpose, Authority and Passion.

First of all, there was a singleness of purpose, a consistency, displayed by Our Lord right through his life, which was bound up with his determination to do the will of his Father. This reached its climax in the Garden of Gethsemane where the great spiritual battle was fought culminating in the words, 'My Father, if it be possible, let this cup pass from me; nevertheless, not as I will, but as thou wilt.'

All through his life there was this identification with the Father and with the will of the Father – 'He who has seen me has seen the Father.' And this was no formal identification, but was achieved through struggle and prayer, even whole nights in prayer.

Here, in one sense, lay Our Lord's greatness in contrast to the greatness of Solomon. Despite his wisdom and possessions, he compromised his kingdom by a variety of external marriages. By his actions the worship of the one true God was also threatened. He lacked that singleness of purpose that characterised Our Lord's greatness.

In the second place, Our Lord's greatness was symbolised by his authority.

There can be a harsh ring about the word authority. We talk today about young people, for example, rebelling against authority as it is perceived in school, parents or church. No doubt part of Solomon's reputation for greatness lay in his authority, the type of authority associated with the many slaves he had.

Contrast that with the authority of Our Lord of whom it was said that 'He taught them as one who had authority and not as their scribes.' In other words, his authority lay not in legalism or external compulsion, but in the love that attracted people and in the deepest sense reflected the very heart of the Divine, for God is love. This was not a formal identification with the Father, but it nonetheless reflected the being of God, which in turn was seen as exhibiting real authority and true greatness, that paradoxical greatness that led to the Cross.

The third mark of greatness is then to be found in the passion of Our Lord, in the victory of the Cross sealed by the resurrection. Here we see love triumphant, not only in enduring to the extent of crucifixion, but rising on the third day victorious. For Solomon death brought an end to his earthly splendour, but for the one greater than Solomon it marked a new beginning, not just in his own personal terms, but in terms of humanity itself through the opening up of a new and living way to the Father.

This is where the true greatness lies, and also the challenge of our faith. So often we identify with the transitory greatness of the Solomons of this world, with what Paul, writing to the Corinthians, calls 'the wisdom of this world.' The challenge is to identify with the one greater than Solomon, for in so doing we begin to experience something of that peace of God which passes understanding.

CHAPTER 32

Matthew Chapter 5 verses 21 and 22 (part):
'You have heard that it was said to the men of old ...
but I say to you'

What was said to the people of old was very direct and specific.
The rules of behaviour and personal relationships were spelled
out clearly in such books as Deuteronomy and Leviticus, and
covered not just the observance of religious festivals such as the
Passover and Day of Atonement, but also the life of the individual in all its most intimate details.

It is a fascinating exercise to read the three Old Testament
books Leviticus, Numbers and Deuteronomy. Apart altogether
from the specific laws dealing with such matters as ritual clean-
liness, personal hygiene, marital and extra-marital relationships
and the punishment for breaking the law, with stoning to death
the most drastic, one can get a feel for the overall atmosphere of
that period which gives insight into much of what Our Lord said
and did.

Take, for example, Our Lord's reference to killing. 'You have
heard that it was said to the men of old, "you shall not kill; and
whosoever kills shall be liable to judgment".' That was a clear
and concise commandment, admittedly expressed in the negative, but reminding the wrongdoer that he would be judged.

There are times when it is necessary to be specific and narrow and condemn those who kill, whether it be those who murder with the bullet and the bomb or those who contribute to the
toll of road deaths in our land.

But the narrow definition, if we are not careful can provide a
form of escapism. 'I would never kill' we say, pointing to those
who bomb or attack the elderly or travel at excessive speed. Yet
are we so exempt? Our Lord did not think so. 'You have heard
that it was said to the men of old you shall not kill. But I say to
you that everyone who is angry with his brother shall be liable
to judgment; whoever insults his brother shall be liable to the

council.' Our Lord took the specific commandments of the old dispensation and gave them a new dimension by expanding and deepening their meaning and application. It is the anger of a hot impulsive heart that so often fathers the foul deed. Killing seldom happens in a vacuum.

These words from Matthew are part of the Sermon on the Mount, that ethical exhortation which has inspired so many people, some of them not Christians. Mahatma Ghandi was said to have lived by its precepts and was encouraged to his life of non-violence.

Sometimes people refer to this famous sermon rather glibly as though what is contained in it can be easily applied. Certainly its precepts must be of universal application if we are to have a world worth living in, but that is not easy.

In the long run it comes down to a sense of personal responsibility, to the individual searching his or her own heart in honesty and being prepared to go out into the world with penitence.

Nowhere is this expressed more clearly than in Chapter 5 verses 23 and 24: 'So if you are offering your gift at the altar, and there remember that your brother has something against you, leave your gift there before the altar and go; first be reconciled to your brother, and then come and offer your gift.' Regularly our gifts are offered at the altar, bread and wine symbolising the work of our hands, money the fruit of our labours, symbols of what we are. As we offer ourselves through these gifts we are challenged to think of our personal relationships, of those with whom we come in contact, of the harsh word, the unkind thought, the poisoned attitude, all that hinders reconciliation.

If we are sincere in our intentions, reconciliation must begin in our own hearts, and where better to do this than at the central act of worship of the church when we bring our gift to the altar.

What was said to the men of old was couched in legalistic and negative terms. The challenge to the followers of Jesus Christ is to live out the universal precepts to which he pointed when he said, 'but I say to you.'

CHAPTER 33

Mark Chapter 3 verses 20 and 21:
'Then he went home, and the crowd came together again, so that they could not even eat. And when his friends heard it, they went out to seize him, for they said, "He is beside himself".'

Friendship is one of the most precious commodities in life. It is, as Samuel Johnston said, 'one of the greatest comforts on this weary pilgrimage.' The person of whom it can be said 'they haven't a friend in the world' is surely one of the most worthy objects of pity.

We are by nature communal beings. It is not good for us to be alone, it is not natural for us to live the hermit-like life. We find the fulfilment of much of our being in relation to other people, the pleasure we enjoy in their company and the sacrifices we make on their behalf. The person who has never sacrificed anything on behalf of another cannot be said to have experienced life in the fullest sense, and one soon realises this if one comes face to face with a thoroughly selfish individual.

The theme of friendship is to be found many times in the bible. Sometimes, as in the Old Testament, the word 'friend' is used in a technical sense as the king's confidential advisor (1 Kgs 4:5). At other times in the bible as a whole it is used as a general greeting. 'Friend, I am doing you no wrong,' were the words of the owner of the vineyard to the labourers when they came for their pay complaining that they had been short changed.

But here and there the thought of friendship becomes much more personal and intimate. In the Old Testament one classic example is the deep-rooted friendship between Jonathan and David, while in the New Testament there is the homely and happy relationship that Our Lord had with Lazarus and his sisters Mary and Martha, whose home in Bethany he resorted to in order to escape from the rush of the city. It was no doubt this type of warm personal friendship that the famous Indian Christian, Bishop Azariah, had in mind when he uttered his memorable plea at the Edinburgh Missionary Conference in 1910: 'Give us friends.' He knew only too well that money and manpower can lose much of their value unless they are undergirded by personal concern, a relationship of friendship between the giver and receiver.

Friendship enriches much of life, and we would all be immeasurably the poorer without our friends. But like everything else even friendship can have its downside, and this is well illustrated by the story from Mark.

Our Lord came to a house and his reputation as a healer had obviously preceded him. So great was the crowd that they could not even eat. When his friends heard of what was happening they came to rescue him, or to 'seize him' as the Revised Standard Version of the bible puts it, for they said 'he is beside himself.' Obviously they thought that they were doing the right thing. Apparently some people were saying that Our Lord was out of his mind and possessed of a devil, and because of this he could heal people of demons. So his well-meaning friends wanted to take charge of him and remove him.

Although so close to him, they did not understand him. This was no devil casting out devils but the power of the living God being manifested. And therein lies the danger that this incident illustrates. Sometimes our friendships blind us so that we fail to appreciate the actions of our friends or we may even misunderstand them.

One of the basic principles of Christianity is that true happiness will only be found in doing the work to which we are called by God. But the call of God can sometimes appear as foolishness in the eyes of the world. It may mean that one's friends begin to say 'he is beside himself.' It has been said on more than one occasion of those who receive a call to the full-time ministry in later life in the midst of a professional career. Sometimes we can be so close in friendship to a person that we fail to understand when a dramatic change takes place in their lives, when they begin to be regulated by a new scale of values. It would be an interesting study to look at those people who have achieved greatness despite their friends. The whole tradition of nursing as we have it today is based on the life of Florence Nightingale who had to stand out against the advice and opinions of her friends. Periodically one meets parents who hold back children from fulfilling a burning ambition, and with the best of intentions attempt to force them into a preconceived pattern of life.

Friendship is indeed a very precious thing, but it can become blind and lacking in perception. Our Lord suffered at the hand of well-meaning friends who no doubt thought that they were doing things for the best. Such is the danger of friendship. True happiness can only be found in doing the will of God. Fortunate the person whose friends help in that fulfilment.

CHAPTER 34

Mark Chapter 10 Verse 51:
'And Jesus said to him, "What do you want me to do for you?"'

The very familiar story of Blind Bartimaeus has many fascinating aspects to it, not least the question put by Jesus to the blind man, 'What do you want me to do for you?'

Our Lord had spent the early part of his ministry in the northern area of Galilee. It was there that his home town of Nazareth was located; where he grew up. There too was the Sea of Galilee where a number of his closest followers had worked as fishermen and Jesus had performed one of his most dramatic miracles in stilling the raging of the sea, a sea notorious for its sudden squalls and storms.

But now he had moved south through the inhospitable country of Samaria, where he had stopped by the well of Sychar and amazed even his disciples by talking to a Samaritan woman. In moving south to Judaea he was returning to the area of his birth, to Bethlehem and the seat of authority, both civil and religious, at Jerusalem. He was moving into that area where his ministry was to come to dramatic fruition through the passion, crucifixion and resurrection.

The incident with Blind Bartimaeus took place at Jericho, a place perhaps more familiar from the Old Testament story of the sounding of the trumpet and the falling down of the walls.

Our Lord was leaving the city with a large crowd. His reputation had followed him from his home area of Galilee, and wherever he went the crowds gathered.

Why did they follow him?

There may have been a genuine regard for what he had to say, for the type of life he advocated which in so many ways ran counter to the legalistic guidelines of the Old Testament. There was a refreshing positive approach in everything Our Lord said and did compared to the negative 'thou shalt not' of the old dispensation.

Or the crowds may have gathered because of Our Lord's personality. 'He spoke as one who had authority' was the way the gospel writers described it. Again, it may have been curiosity at this miracle worker, and the hope that they might actually see a miracle performed. There may even have been a political motive. Was this possibly the one who would lead the country out of subjection to the might of the Roman Empire? Whatever the reason, the crowds followed him.

But crowds pose their own problems and they are not all a matter of physical control. A problem arises when members of the crowd feel that they have a prior call on the time and attention of the central character and become offended when anyone else intrudes.

This was the case as Jesus and his disciples and the large crowd left Jericho. In this case the intruder was a blind beggar. Beggars can be persistent, as anyone who walks the streets of any city soon finds out. But sometimes persistence is the only approach. Nor is it one discounted in the bible. Importunity paid off for the man who came looking for food at midnight in the gospel story. Knock, keep knocking, and it shall be opened. Ask, keep on asking, and ye shall receive. This was the advice given by Our Lord.

Do we sometimes give up too easily in an age where instant solutions are the order of the day? Do we give up too easily in our prayers if we don't get the desired response? In any branch of life there is great merit in stickability. And Our Lord seems to be saying this in terms of our relationship with him; don't give up when things appear to be at a standstill, keep on praying, calling, knocking, asking.

So it was with Bartimaeus. He kept on calling out despite the efforts of those closest to Jesus to keep him quiet. And his persistence paid off. Jesus stopped and said, 'call him'. And when he came Our Lord put the question, 'What do you want me to do for you?' The man responded in terms of his immediate and personal perceived needs, 'Master, let me receive my sight', and immediately Jesus healed him. The question put by Jesus is still the leading question, 'What do you want me to do for you?' For most people it is not a question of physical blindness. So much can be done today that was not possible in Our Lord's day. But for many there is still a blindness nonetheless. The way it is described in the Letter to the Ephesians is, 'They are darkened in their understanding'. And so in response to the recurring question of Jesus the repeated answer must still be, 'Master, let me receive my sight'. Let me receive my sight in order that I may see my own weakness. It is only in acknowledging my own weakness, my own sinfulness, that I can begin to be helped and come to a realisation of the goodness, mercy and forgiveness of God.

Let me receive my sight in order that I may see Christ in the world, especially in the needs of others, the homeless, the unemployed, the sexually abused, the poor, the casualties of marriage breakdown.

If the request to receive our sight is made in sincerity and truth, the answer will come today just as surely as it came to Bartimaeus – 'immediately he received his sight'.

But there was an important sequel. The response of Bartimaeus was that he followed Jesus on the way. He committed himself to the one who had healed him. And that surely must be the response of all those whose sight has been restored.

CHAPTER 35

Mark Chapter 16 verse 18:
'They will lay hands on the sick; and they will recover.'

The practice of the laying on of hands is of very ancient origin. In the very first book of the bible we read that Jacob blessed Joseph's two sons, Ephraim and Manasseh, by placing his hands on their heads. Later it was used as a means of setting people apart for a specific purpose, as when Moses laid his hands on Joshua to invest him with a measure of authority.

In the New Testament, the laying on of hands became identified with what we now understand as confirmation and ordination.

However, early on the practice came to be linked with ministry to the sick, and today those who exercise this ministry are complying with the directive given by Our Lord to his followers after the resurrection, 'they will lay hands on the sick and they will recover.' There are at least three points to consider in relation to the laying on of hands.

1. First and foremost, it is a means or channel of grace. True, there is the human element involved in that the hands are human hands, and this poses a danger.

We live in an age of the personality cult. Individuals are glorified and glamourised, whether they be sports personalities, pop stars, or more local celebrities. So with the laying on of hands, it must always be a case of 'not I, but the grace of God'. Paul, in writing to the Corinthians, stressed this over and over again. His underlying theme was, 'By the grace of God I am what I am.' Those who minister the laying on of hands must always see themselves, and be seen by others, as instruments or channels of God's grace, a thought expressed so well in the modern version of the prayer of St Francis, 'Make me a channel of your peace'.

2. In the second place, the laying on of hands calls for penitence and self-examination, and it does so in order that the obstacles to the grace of God may be removed.

It is not without significance that at the start of all our regular services there is this element of penitence when we seek to open our hearts to God for his cleansing. It's a process wonderfully expressed in the familiar collect for purity, 'Almighty God unto whom all hearts are open ... cleanse the thoughts of our hearts ...'

As a prelude to the laying on of hands there is no more suitable preparation than the prayer for purity. Some use the commandments, combining them with the New Testament summary as it is contained in the *Alternative Prayer Book*. 'Thou shalt not' is counterbalanced by Our Lord's positive interpretation in each case. Whatever is used it is important to come prepared for the laying on of hands, so that we who are frail human beings may be ready and prepared, like the five wise virgins with their lamps trimmed, to greet the Lord when he comes.

3. Thirdly, it has been found helpful by many people to come for the laying on of hands with a specific intention in relation to healing, whether it be for themselves, another person, a relationship that needs renewal or a distorted attitude that can so easily lead to unjustified prejudice. In other words, it is important to focus the mind on some specific area, trusting that the grace of God will uplift and renew. The ministry of healing has to do, not just with individual physical illness, but also with attitudes and relationships that can often, quite literally, be soul destroying. 'Fear not then,' said Our Lord, 'who only destroy the body, but fear them that can destroy both soul and body.'

In this context it is important to draw a distinction between curing and healing. Healing is a much deeper and more comprehensive process than curing. We cannot deny that God cures illness, and there are many who can testify to this fact. But there are countless others who, in the midst of pain and suffering, have found a healing peace. The undoubted problem of suffering which agitates so many people is counterbalanced by the mystery of serenity, sometimes in the midst of great physical distress. God uses the ministry of the laying on of hands in a variety of ways to bring his healing, and the title Ministry of Healing is well chosen.

CHAPTER 36

Mark Chapter 3 verses 13-15:
'And he went up into the hills, and called to him
those whom he desired; and they came to him.
And he appointed twelve to be with him, and to be sent out
to preach and have authority to cast out demons.'

'Vocation' and 'ministry' are two words often heard together in the context of ordination. Occasionally, when it is feared that the flow of ordinands is drying up, the church is encouraged to have a vocation and ministry Sunday.

But what is involved in vocation and ministry? We can learn much by turning to the call of 'the twelve' in Mark. 'And he went up into the hills, and called to him those whom he desired.'

The vocation or call to the ministry is always God's call, and where it is not (as sometimes happened in the past with well-meaning parents) it becomes an intolerable burden. Just as there is no more fulfilling life than that of the ordained ministry, so too there is no life more miserable than that of a mistaken ordinand. God calls those whom he desires. The church does not create vocation, but it should provide the setting and atmosphere in which the call can be heard. It is also the task of the church to test the vocation of those who feel called, in order that the call may be authenticated.

This places an onus on the church and on each parish to be the type of setting in which vocation is affirmed and encouraged. But so often we are engaged in what J. V. Taylor, in *The Go Between God*, describes as 'the demented activism of these days'. The result is that vocation is stifled. George Appleton, in *The Word is the Seed*, reminds his readers that the Spirit of God can act wherever the spirit of man is 'awake and receptive'. It is the responsibility of the church to provide the stimulation to bring this about.

The call of God must be answered, there must be a response. And that is what happened in Mark's account, 'they came to him'. Those who went into the hills in response to the summons of Jesus were, in a sense, going into the unknown. In this passage, immediately preceding this verse, there is the incident of the unclean spirits crying out to Jesus, 'You are the Son of God', and his strict order to them not to make him known. In hindsight as we read the gospel we can know something of the person who called those whom he desired. But for those who responded at that time there was an unknown element that necessitated faith and trust.

Invariably it is like this when God calls. We are encouraged to take one step at a time, not to be over anxious for the morrow, but to respond to the limited vision we may have received. If we seek to have all the spiritual i's dotted and t's crossed we will never respond. Indeed sometimes it may be better for us not to have the full scope of God's call before us. 'If I knew what was involved I would never have taken it on.' How often we hear those words, and maybe have uttered them ourselves. They are not without relevance in the sphere of vocation.

Mark goes on to tell us that 'they came to him. And he appointed twelve.'

From those who responded to the call a particular group was set apart for certain work. This does not mean that the remainder were simply cast to one side on the scrapheap. Within the church we take a very narrow view of ministry if we confine it to the work of those who have been ordained. The writer of the Letter to the Ephesians reminds us that some are called to be apostles, prophets, evangelists, pastors and teachers. In other words there is a variety of ministry and God has a purpose for each one. He calls each one to service in some capacity, and this is the basic meaning of ministry.

And so we must ask constantly what is God calling me to do, in this situation, at this time? The call of God is always contemporary because he is the living God, God active in human affairs.

'He appointed twelve, to be with him, and to be sent out.'

For some the call of God is to the ordained ministry, just as some were called to serve in a particular capacity with Jesus.

They were to be with him, to be identified with him and to be his representatives. 'Are you not also one of this man's followers?' The question was put to Peter because he was recognised as having been with Jesus. But not only were the twelve appointed to be with Jesus, they were also to be sent out. They were to be apostles.

To be with Jesus and to be sent out, this twofold aspect is still at the heart of ordained ministry today. Those called to this work, if they are to be true to their calling, must stay close to Jesus, and this element is embraced in the ordination service where those being ordained are enjoined to be diligent in prayer and bible study. The words of C.S. Lewis are very relevant: 'A man cannot always be defending the truth, there must be a time to feed on it.'

However, the ordained ministry is not intended to be a hot-house existence. Authority is given by the church through the bishop to preach, to seek out the sick and unbaptised, and to promote peace and reconciliation. It is a reflection of Our Lord's commission to the twelve to be sent out as ambassadors. Those who respond to the call of God will be given work to do, work for which they will draw their inspiration from Jesus himself, work which may well lead them into uncharted territory.

CHAPTER 37

Luke Chapter 2 verse 4:
'And Joseph also went up from Galilee,
from the city of Nazareth, to Judea, to the city of David, which
is called Bethlehem'

The Bethlehem story is about the best known story in the bible. Yet often it is the least understood because of what we have made of it in the intervening years.

To stand in Manger Square in Bethlehem is to run the risk of being mown down by a tourist bus, not to mention the persistent souvenir sellers. Inside the Church of the Nativity, as one contemplates the ornate setting of the traditional site of the manger, it is difficult to visualise the scene as it is depicted in so many hymns and carols – the cattle lowing as the baby awakes.

Of course it would be foolish to imagine that time can or should stand still. But the modern traditional site of the manger is symbolic of a much deeper change that has taken place in society at large. In his first Christmas message as the new secretary of the Anglican Communion, John L Peterson spoke of the Christmas event as the Divine Reversal. Having served for twelve years as Dean of St George's College, Jerusalem, he had more opportunities than most to imbibe the atmosphere of the Holy Land. Going back to the announcement of Our Lord's birth he wrote, 'One of the things that always stands out in my mind every time I am in Nazareth is that first-century Nazareth was an insignificant unwalled town, not even on a major road. The major city of the Galilee at the time of Jesus' birth was Sepphoris, located some six kilometres north of Nazareth. Any important announcement would have been made in Sepphoris, the seat of government. No one would ever have thought about making any announcement in Nazareth. But it is in Nazareth that God chose to make the greatest announcement of all time.' And he goes on to say, 'I like to think of this as the Divine Reversal, God turning upside down everything that we hold to be so important:

power, prestige, wealth. God chose Nazareth to make the greatest announcement of all time. According to the standards of the world, God should have chosen Sepphoris.'

Could we not say the same of Bethlehem, the setting in which God chose to reveal himself to humanity? Think of this in relation to modern attitudes.

Bethlehem represents humility, the self-emptying of God who made himself of no reputation and took the form of a servant. Bethlehem represents weakness, the total incapacity of an infant, dependent on others for his very survival.

Bethlehem represents the extraordinary in contrast to the mundane, the breaking through of the Divine, with its challenge to our persistent longing for proof and credibility. It is a challenge to our faith, just as it was to the faith of Mary. Her first reaction on being told of the future birth was, 'How can this be?' Yet her faith shines through in her acceptance of God's will, 'I am the Lord's servant, may it be to me as you have said.'

Bethlehem represents the greatest bridge-building exercise the world has ever known, a unique event, the restoration of the relationship between the Divine and the human.

Think then of all that Bethlehem stands for – humility, dependence, simplicity, faith, bridge building – and then ask how far it reflects today's world?

If the first Christmas Day was the unique revelation of God to the world, then surely we must take careful note of the manner of that revelation, and seek to reflect something of its characteristics in our lives. Not an easy task when humility and dependence and simplicity can so easily be interpreted as weakness. Yet, like it or not, these are the qualities at the heart of Christian living, reflecting the words of Paul to the Corinthians, 'But God chose what is foolish in the world to shame the wise; God chose what is weak in the world to shame the strong; God chose what is low and despised in the world, things that are not, to reduce to nothing things that are, so that no one might boast in the presence of God' (1 Cor 1:27-29).

But it is in the realm of bridge-building that the incarnation speaks most directly, and provides the inspiration for those working for peace throughout the world, and not least in our own country. Our prayer must be that God's initiative, in stretching out to sinful humanity, will be reflected in the coming together in peace of those for so long severed by strife. May the miracle of Bethlehem be reflected in the world of the new millennium.

CHAPTER 38

Luke Chapter 8 verses 1-3:
'Soon afterwards he went on through cities and villages,
preaching and bringing the good news of the kingdom of God.
And the twelve were with him, and also some of the women
who had been healed of evil spirits and infirmities: Mary, called
Magdalene, from whom seven demons had gone out, and
Joanna, the wife of Chuza, Herod's steward, and Susanna, and
many others, who provided for them out of their means.'

'I would like to hear a sermon on the women who helped Jesus
and the disciples, and provided for them out of their means.'
Such was one of the requests received in response to a parish
questionnaire on preaching. It read like a 'Jim'll fix it' letter.

In this context the opening verses of Luke 8 set the scene and
are a reminder that the gospel according to St Luke has been
called the Gospel of Womanhood because of the way in which
Our Lord's gracious and tender dealings with a number of
women is recorded. In addition, the first two chapters of the
book provide details of his early life which must surely have
come from the Virgin Mary.

The first few words of the text indicate a new departure in
Our Lord's method of action. Up to this he had made Caper-
naum his headquarters, and had not moved very far from there.
Now he was beginning a wider range of mission, and this
brought with it obvious problems of maintenance and adminis-
tration, or logistics as we would say in our modern jargon. How
were Jesus and the twelve to survive as they went from place to
place? Luke, in this short passage, which he alone records, tells
that certain women who had been healed of evil spirits and
infirmities ministered to them of their substance. He mentions
three in particular – Mary Magdalene, or Mary of Magdala, to
distinguish her from the many other Marys; Joanna, the wife of
Herod's steward, which may account for the origin of Luke's
special knowledge of Herod's court which he displays in the
passion narrative; and Susanna, which means 'Lily'.

There are at least two interesting factors indicated by these verses.

In the first place we are made aware of the practical problems involved in Our Lord's ministry. It is the human side breaking through. And it was solved by the womenfolk, as is so often the case. Such a large group could not be expected to rely on casual hospitality alone.

One commentator makes the point that these verses are deeply interesting as throwing light on the otherwise unsolved problem of the means of livelihood possessed by Jesus and the apostles. They had a common purse which served both their own needs and those of the poor. And he goes on to say that the apostles had absolutely forsaken their daily callings, but it may be supposed that a few of them (like Matthew and the sons of the wealthy fisherman, Zebedee) had resources of their own, but here we see that these women, some of whom were rich, helped to maintain the group. However, this same commentator goes on to make the point that their needs would have been comparatively meagre or small. Ordinary maintenance in the Palestine of the first century would have been far removed from what sophisticated Western society would look on as necessary today.

In the second place, and perhaps of more significance, is the fact that the womenfolk were involved at all. At that time the Scribes and Pharisees gathered up their robes in the streets and synagogues lest they should touch a woman. Even the disciples themselves, when they found Jesus talking to the Samaritan woman at the well of Sychar, appear to have been more concerned that he was talking to a woman than to a Samaritan – 'They were astonished that he was speaking with a woman' (Jn 4:27). But here Jesus was reminding his followers in a very direct way of something Paul underlined, that in Christ there is neither male nor female.

The sequel to these verses is found in the fact that these same women stayed with Our Lord to the end. They were with him at the crucifixion. They came to the tomb bringing spices. Their devotion was no passing phase, but was obviously born out of deep commitment and a willingness to serve. Other women, especially as recorded by Luke, flit in and out of the picture. Even Mary and Martha, in their settled home at Bethany, while important as providing a place of refuge for Our Lord, are in a sense incidental. But this band of women occupied a special place in the ministry of Our Lord and his apostles. That there was not greater recorded opposition to what they did is quite remarkable given the cultural background of the first century.

At a time when the role of women in society is so much under discussion, not least the role of women in the church, it is appropriate to look afresh at the part played by women in the ministry of Our Lord, not least those who provided for him out of their means, and were his constant companions at the most harrowing period of his ministry.

CHAPTER 39

Luke Chapter 11 verse 23:
'He who is not with me is against me'

When we look back into the Old Testament we see conflict writ large on its pages. The followers of the God of Abraham, Isaac and Jacob fought a constant battle with forces representing the false gods of their day. The contest between David and Goliath is a symbolic example of that conflict. Yet through the conflict God was seen to be working his purpose.

In the epistles of the New Testament we are constantly reminded that in the spiritual sphere there is a recurring conflict between the spirit of Christ and the spirit of anti-Christ, the spirit of truth and the spirit of error, the prophets of God and the many false prophets that abound. As John says (1 Jn 4:1), 'Beloved, do not believe every spirit, but test the spirits to see whether they are of God; for many false prophets have gone out into the world.' This is good advise to the spiritually naïve who can easily be misled by sweet words.

Turning to the gospels we see Our Lord reminding his hearers that conflict can lead to disaster: 'Every kingdom divided against itself becomes a desert, and house falls on house' (Lk 11:17). And he underlined this in a very personal way by saying, 'He who is not with me is against me.'

In the bible conflict is a reality, and the lesson must be that allegiance to God is no guarantee of an escape from that conflict. Indeed quite the contrary, as the experience of so many people down through history has proved – Terry Waite, a hostage for 1763 days as he pursued political truth; Pastor Dietrich Bonhoeffer, executed for his stand opposing the evil of the Hitler regime; Martin Luther King, assassinated because of his stand for civil rights; Archbishop Janani Luwum, murdered because of his opposition to political injustice. They all suffered because in varying ways they were at the centre of conflict between light and darkness, goodness and evil.

But it might be said that these were all famous names, leaders in their respective spheres of work, and such people tend to get caught up in more obvious conflict by reason of their position in life. And to an extent this is true, but only up to a point. For example, it was said of Archbishop Luwum that he was a man who never hid the truth, and he died because he always sought to bring everything into the light. This must surely be the vocation of every Christian, never to hide the truth, to live in the light.

To some that may seem a rather abstract comment to make, pious-sounding advice. But try relating it to home and work and leisure, to all our relationships. What it is really challenging us to do is test our standards by the life and mind of Christ who himself said, 'I am the way, the truth and the life' and 'I am the light of the world.'

However, the uncomfortable fact is that we so often tend to gravitate towards the darkness rather than the light, and this is where the inner conflict enters in as we seek to live by the truth. There is an inevitable conflict once we have committed ourselves to Jesus Christ. It is not conflict for the sake of conflict, but rather the tension that arises when light and darkness, truth and falsehood, goodness and evil come face to face.

Never to have experienced this conflict throws in question the whole nature of one's commitment to Christ. There can be no sitting on the fence. There is no such thing as a neutral Christian. As Our Lord himself said, 'He who is not with me is against me.'

CHAPTER 40

Luke Chapter 19 verses 1-2:
'He entered Jericho and was passing through it.
A man was there named Zacchaeus;
he was a chief tax-collector and was rich.'

The story of Zacchaeus is one of those once-off stories that sticks in the mind. On returning from a trip to the Holy Land a few years ago one of the first questions put to me by my four year old grandson was, 'did you see Zacchaeus?' He had just heard the story in school and it made an immediate impact. It is found only in Luke, and Zacchaeus himself is mentioned nowhere else in the bible. However, on the basis that nothing appears in the bible without some purpose, what can be said about the story?

In the first place, Zacchaeus was rich, and in the New Testament we are told, not that riches will exclude people from the kingdom of God, but they will make it more difficult to enter. Today's affluent society tends to promote an exaggerated sense of self-sufficiency, which is far removed from that attitude of humility which is one of the hallmarks of Christianity. Yet, despite his riches, Zacchaeus sought Jesus with obvious enthusiasm.

In the second place, we note that Zacchaeus was part of a crowd, part of the multitude that gathered wherever Jesus appeared.

But one of the characteristics of the crowds that followed Jesus was that, despite the multitudes, he noticed individuals. And so it was with Zacchaeus. It is easy to feel lost in the crowd. Yet at the heart of the Christian Faith is belief in the value and importance of the individual. It is the privilege of each person to be able to say, Christ died for me. This thought is expressed in simple language in one of our delightful children's hymns:

God who made the earth
The air, the sky, the sea,
Who gave the light its birth,
Careth for me.

But not only did Jesus notice Zacchaeus and pick him out in the crowd, he called him by name. In doing this he gave him individual standing. He was not just a statistic, but had an identity. We all know how pleased we feel when someone remembers our name. It indicates a real interest, that an effort has been made.

However, having called Zacchaeus by name Jesus then made a demand upon him: 'Zacchaeus, hurry and come down; for I must stay at your house today.' It is easy to imagine the problems that such a request would pose, not least from a domestic point of view. But in addition there was the prejudice of Our Lord's followers as they accused him of going to be a guest with a sinner. No doubt the other side of the coin would have been represented by Zacchaeus's friends, equally suspicious at him consorting with this strange preacher.

But when the call to follow Jesus comes there is invariably a demand made as well. That is the overall lesson of the gospel and not just of this particular incident. 'Sell what you have and give to the poor,' was Our Lord's advice to the rich young man who sought the route to eternal life. The lawyer who came with the same question was challenged to love God and his neighbour. To James and John the challenge was equally forthright when they sought the privileged positions in the kingdom. Could they drink the same cup as Our Lord? Always there is a demand when a commitment is made. What that demand may be at any given time, in any given situation and for any given individual, is not easy to define. But it always demands thought and heartsearching. Indeed if one has never had to make any agonising appraisals in relation to life, then the Christian commitment involved will most certainly have been superficial.

The postscript to the story of Zacchaeus is that, despite the comments and demands, he received Jesus joyfully and was rewarded with the assurance, 'Today salvation has come to this house.'

CHAPTER 41

Luke Chapter 11 verse 1:
'Lord teach us to pray'

This request of the disciples to Our Lord is one which has ever been at the heart of Christian experience, and at no time more so than the present. The growth of prayer groups and the interest in meditation are reminders that at the heart of human experience is a longing to commune with the Divine. Prayer has well been described as 'the oxygen of the soul', for without it the spiritual life withers and decays.

But first of all, what do we mean by praying? Let me stick out my neck and give a short definition, 'conversing with God'. I use the word conversing rather than talking, because it conveys the idea of two-way traffic, of listening as well as talking. The Irish are noted talkers. We have even coined a name to describe this activity, 'craic', one of the selling points of the tourist board, while in Cork there is a industry built round it with the Blarney Stone.

On a recent radio programme the speaker referred to God as a friend. 'I rely on God as a friend' was the way it was expressed. It's a good image to have of God in the context of prayer because it reminds us of some of the essential elements in the Divine/-human relationship. Let me mention some of them.

(1) A true friend is one to whom we are prepared to give time. When we are in their company there is no sense of watching the clock. We are happy to stay and chat. We make time to be with them.

And so it is with prayer. Time is an essential ingredient if we want to develop a prayerful attitude. To rescue time (or as the bible puts it, 'to redeem the time') from the fast flowing stream of life demands discipline. But it is worth the effort. It can be done on an ever-expanding basis, built into the rhythm of the day. Begin with just a few moments and build on that foundation, just as an athlete builds up stamina over a lengthy period.

It is surprising how this prayer period can become a part of the daily routine, just like reading the paper or watching *Glenroe.* What is important is to make a start.

(2) Our friends are those to whom we turn, but not just in times of need. We are happy to be in their company and to share their fellowship.

So too it must be with our praying. Of course it is right that we should come to God with our needs – 'Ask and you will receive'; 'Come to me all you that are weary and are carrying heavy burdens, and I will give you rest.' It is this assurance of the mercy and goodness of God that so often makes life bearable. But to come only at times of crisis, as to a social welfare agency, is to divest our prayer of such joyful elements as adoration and thanksgiving. It is to limit the scope of our prayers unnecessarily.

(3) With our true friends we drop all pretence, we can be ourselves. The relationship is one of openness.

And this must be our attitude to God in prayer. The story of the contrasting attitudes of the Pharisee and the Publican at prayer is a stark reminder of the necessity for honesty in approaching God – 'God be merciful to me, a sinner'; 'Nothing in my hand I bring'. Yet because we live in a society of so much pretence this is not an easy attitude to cultivate. So many people put on an act or lead a type of Jekyll and Hyde existence. It is part of the mood of the modern age. But in coming to God as a friend in prayer we must drop the veil of pretence. As we do this not only will our relationship with God deepen, but we will begin to experience a renewed sense of freedom and authenticity in all our relationships. A wonderful way of achieving this is through regular use of the collect for purity in the Communion service: 'Almighty God to whom all hearts are open.'

(4) True friendship involves listening. 'So-and-so is a good listener' we sometimes say in a complimentary sense. It can happen that we become so adept at talking that we lose the art of listening.

So it is with prayer. We feel that we must fill the time with words – our words – and the voice of God is drowned out. One of our well known hymns catches the mood:

'Speak Lord in the stillness while I wait on thee,

Hushed my soul to silence in expectancy.'

Or the words of the psalmist: 'Be still and know that I am God'.

One of my favourite prayer tapes is by a famous Methodist minister, Frank Topping. It is an imaginary telephone conversation between 'Ginger Kelly' and God. God is being told off for being engaged when Ginger tried to get through to him yesterday. What had happened was that Ginger had talked so much he didn't hear God replying. In the Church of Ireland liturgical tradition of worship, silence is not something we use very much, but it can and should be a part of our private prayers. It gives God a chance.

(5) At the end of the day friendship is more than a series of identifiable factors as outlined above. And in a similar manner prayer is more than just saying prayers. It is an attitude to life which can see the divine writ large in everyday objects and events. We have a very good example of this in Michel Quoist's *Prayers of Life,* where he uses as a basis for prayer such mundane objects as a five pound note, a blackboard and a tractor. In the Irish context we have a notable example in Joseph Plunkett's lovely poem:

I see his blood upon the rose

And in the stars the glory of his eyes.

Start to pray then by thinking of God as a friend and approaching him as such. Don't be unduly worried about the words. True friends can often communicate without speaking. You will be surprised at how the friendship develops. Or to express it in another way – learn to pray by praying.

CHAPTER 42

Luke Chapter 23 verse 34:
'Father, forgive them; for they do not know what they are doing.'

Few passages in the bible seem to represent a more truly Christian outlook than this first word from the cross: 'Father forgive them …' The concept of forgiveness is at the heart of the Christian Faith – 'He died that we might be forgiven.' It is at the heart of the prayer that binds all Christians together as one family – 'Forgive us our trespasses as we forgive those who trespass against us.' Students of that period of church history tell us that the word of forgiveness was uttered before the Cross was actually raised on high, as Our Lord was being nailed and fastened to the beams.

At such a time of sheer physical pain, a captive would have been expected to blaspheme and curse his captors. It was a cruel death, used as a deterrent for wrong doers. In addition, Calvary was a very public place and the taunting jests of the crowd, together with the gruff and unsympathetic manner of the soldiers, would heighten the atmosphere of dejection.

Yet it was in such an unlikely situation that the word of forgiveness was spoken, and it is important to realise this in order to understand the depth of its meaning.

One of the remarkable features of Our Lord's bearing on the Cross was his thought for others, and here in this first word we see it most plainly illustrated.

'Father forgive them.' To whom was Our Lord referring when he said this?

The soldiers? In one sense the soldiers bore less of the blame than many others. They were the final actors to come on stage during the drama of the passion. The drama could not have reached this point without the involvement of other characters.

Pilate, the Roman governor? Here was a man of authority, representing the most powerful regime of the day. Perhaps he was ambitious for promotion, and as Caesar's son-in-law his prospects were good. Perhaps he was anxious to avoid crowd trouble with huge numbers in Jerusalem for the Passover. Perhaps he was weak, bowing to pressure – 'If you release this man, you are no friend of the emperor.' Whatever the reason, he gave Our Lord to be crucified despite his own judgment – 'I find no case against him.'

Judas Iscariot? Here was the member of the inner band who betrayed Our Lord for thirty pieces of silver.

Judas may simply have been greedy. He was after all treasurer of the band of disciples. Or he may have been impatient and anxious for action, dissatisfied with Our Lord's method of peaceful persuasion. He wanted results and he wanted them now, and so he tried to force Our Lord's hand by betraying him, hoping that he would react in a militant fashion.

Caiaphas, the high priest? Here was a man of immense power, holding the people in his grasp, described as a snake waiting the opportune moment to strike. The office of high priest had become deeply tainted with political intrigue, and experience teaches that the mixture of religion and politics can be lethal.

The Crowd? Shouting 'Crucify him, Crucify him' they were easily swayed by the cunning of Caiaphas and the emotion of the moment. Speaking out of a volatile situation, a former Archbishop of Cape Town, Joost de Blank, once said, 'The blood lust of people is perhaps the most vicious of all emotions.'

A variety of people in their own way helped to nail Our Lord to the Cross. Surely it was for all of these that he uttered the word of forgiveness. But that word is an eternal word, spoken for all those who see their lives mirrored in the personalities of the passion – in the acquiescence of the soldiers, the ambition of Pilate, the greed and impatience of Judas, the misused authority of Caiaphas, the blind emotion of the crowd.

As we come in penitence to the foot of the Cross, and as we acknowledge and cast our burden on the Lord, we can all hear afresh this word of comfort – 'Father, forgive them, for they do not know what they are doing.'

CHAPTER 43

Luke Chapter 24 verse 31:
'Then their eyes were opened, and they recognised him;
and he vanished from their sight.'

There is no more appropriate day on which to be confirmed than Easter Day. The faith confirmed by the laying on of hands is based on the fact of the resurrection. When faith is assailed by doubt, when darkness seems to have overcome the light, when evil appears to have gained the upperhand and good to have been suppressed, at such times we look to the resurrection and faith is renewed, hope restored and joy rekindled. The Easter greeting, 'Christ is risen', and the response, 'The Lord is risen indeed, Alleluia' give the scriptural undergirding to all this.

But Easter Day is not just appropriate in historical terms, it is also appropriate from a personal point of view. To be confirmed on Easter Day is to ensure that it will be pinpointed in all future years. Most people probably recall something about their confirmation, but an Easter confirmation makes it extra memorable. The day enhances the occasion.

A well-known event on the evening of the first Easter day has much to teach us in the context of confirmation. It is the story of the two disciples on the road to Emmaus.

They were discussing the events that had taken place in Jerusalem when they were joined by Jesus. In a fascinating way he drew them out. He then conducted a period of bible study, 'beginning with Moses and all the prophets, he interpreted to them the things about himself in all the scriptures.' When they reached Emmaus the two travellers invited Jesus to join them for a meal, and it was during the meal that he was made known to them in the breaking of bread. Then we read, 'their eyes were opened, and they recognised him; and he vanished from their sight.'

In the context of a confirmation service, there are four brief comments that can be made about this incident.

(1) The story is about a journey. In a sense we are all on a journey, a spiritual journey, which begins at baptism and continues all through life. Confirmation is a special stage on that journey, what is sometimes called a growth point.

(2) The Emmaus journey involved a course of bible study, and for those on their Christian pilgrimage the use of the bible is specifically enjoined at confirmation. Through the reading of the scriptures we are enabled to grow in the faith.

(3) The journey ended with a meal, and in this way Jesus became known to his fellow travellers. 'The Breaking of Bread' is one of the titles by which Holy Communion is known, and this action is still an integral part of the service. Again, this is one of the ways by which Christ is still made known to us. But there is an onus on us to come to this meal regularly, to come prepared and with anticipation. Do we always come with a sense of expectation to the worship of Almighty God?

(4) The fourth observation is perhaps a little surprising and is contained in the words, 'Then their eyes were opened, and they recognised him; and he vanished from their sight.' There are times when our Christian faith is very real, when we are conscious of the presence of God in our lives and of our relationship with Jesus Christ. It may be at worship, in the presence of friends, when close to nature or viewing a beautiful sunset. But there are also times when, as with the two travellers, Christ seems to have vanished from our sight. It may be at times of undeserved tragedy, sickness, national violence or world hunger. At such times the poignant cry from the Cross is very real, 'My God, my God, why have you forsaken me?' It is on such occasions that our faith comes into play, that we hold fast to the resurrection. It is because of this that Christians are sometimes described as Easter people.

And so what better way for confirmation candidates to think of themselves, especially on Easter Day? From now on they will be Easter people in a very special way.

CHAPTER 44

John Chapter 1 verse 5:
'The light shines in the darkness.'

'The most profound book ever written' is a description which has been applied to the gospel according to St. John. The opening words or prologue are among the most familiar in the bible, containing that great message of hope: 'The light shines in the darkness, and the darkness did not overcome it', or as it is expressed in the New English Bible, 'the darkness has never mastered it'.

It is this hope which is at the heart of the Christian faith. The darkness that was present at the crucifixion was but the prelude to the resurrection. The risen life of Christ is the light of the world, and in so far as the life of Christ is in us we shine forth to humanity reflecting him who is the way, the truth and the life. There is a wealth of meaning in the children's hymn, 'Jesus bids us shine', which we as adults may not always appreciate. But we can only shine in so far as Jesus shines through us, in so far as we lose our identity and reflect his.

On All Saints' Day our thoughts turn towards the great multitude in every generation who have reflected and are reflecting Christ in their lives. This is what sainthood is all about. The trouble is that we have hedged it round with notions of perfection, not allowing for the fact that there are many stages on the road to perfection, a destination which we can never reach in this life. Even more than that, we have tended to think of saintliness as something weak and sentimental, divorced from the realities of life, forgetting that it is in the midst of life with its trials, temptations, setbacks and disappointments that saintliness is nurtured. Indeed it is often only against such a background that the true worth of a person emerges, reflecting the thought of William Temple that a person will never know what their faith is worth until some severe test comes.

And so on All Saints' day in our remembrances we do not

limit ourselves, but we give thanks for all those in every generation and in every walk of life who have reflected the light of Christ in their lives, those who, to quote Jeremy Taylor, have been 'fellow workers with God in the laboratories of salvation.'

One of the characteristics of the saints is the variety of their deeds and virtues. We must not limit our horizons in this respect and confine saintliness to actions associated with church buildings. Think of a mother who for twelve years brought her invalid son to hospital every week, or the retired shipyard worker in Belfast who every day without fail brought his pal in a wheelchair for a walk until death parted them, or the teenage girl visiting an elderly lady in a nursing home week after week. Such people would be taken aback if described as saints, but such is the stuff of sainthood. Well may we pray in the words of the collect of this day:

'Give us grace to follow your blessed saints
in all virtuous and godly living.'

CHAPTER 45

John Chapter 3 verse 7:
'You must be born from above.'

Few texts from scripture are more frequently used than this phrase from John, perhaps more familiar in the Authorised Version, 'Ye must be born again'. Indeed at times it appears to be overused. But overuse in one quarter should not lead to underuse in other quarters, because the words and their context are of vital significance.

To look first at the context:

'Now there was a Pharisee named Nicodemus, a leader of the Jews. He came to Jesus by night.'

Nicodemus was a wealthy man. At the time of the crucifixion we read that he brought a mixture of myrrh and aloes, about a hundred pound weight, for Our Lord's body. To have been in a position to do this he must have been a man of substance. He was also a Pharisee, and as such would have separated himself from all ordinary life in order to keep every detail of the law. We know that Jesus had some very harsh things to say about this very legalistic attitude to life, and so it was all the more remarkable that Nicodemus would want to talk to Jesus.

But not only was Nicodemus a Pharisee, he was also a member of the Jewish ruling council, the Sanhedrin, the supreme inner court of seventy, who amongst other tasks dealt with any Jew suspected of being a false prophet. This makes it even more astonishing that he came to Jesus, and possibly explains why the visit was nocturnal. It is easy to condemn him for not coming out into the open, but given his whole background it is quite amazing that he came at all. There must have been some pressing questions he wanted to discuss.

He began with a little diplomatic flattery – 'Rabbi, we know that you are a teacher who has come from God; for no one can do these signs that you do apart from the presence of God.' To this Jesus replies, 'Very truly, I tell you, no one can see the king-

dom of God without being born from above.' In other words,
Jesus was saying that what mattered was not really the miracul-
ous signs but rather that radical change in a person's heart that
could only be described as being 'born from above' or 'born
again'. This thought was not immediately obvious to Nicodemus who interpreted the words in a quite literal sense, and
responded by asking, 'How can anyone be born after having
grown old? Can one enter a second time into the mother's womb
and be born?' The ambiguity arose because the same word, *anwqen*
(anothen), in Greek conveys the two meanings – being born radically from above, i.e. from God, and literally being born again in
a physical sense. Nicodemus latched on to the second thought,
literal rebirth. But Jesus reminded him of the other interpretation, and stressed that no one can enter the kingdom of God
without being born of water and Spirit (Jn 3:5).

Being born of water and Spirit has a twofold thrust. Water is
the symbol of cleansing and the Spirit is the symbol of power,
the washing away of past sinfulness and the hope of victory in
the future. Expressed in another way, water signifies the conscious turning to God known as repentance, the deliberate turning of our backs on the past and facing the opposite direction,
and the Spirit signifies the new strength which comes to us, en-
abling us to be what we set out to be, and to do what by ourselves we could never do.

This whole process is set in train at baptism. There we say of
the newly baptised infant, 'Father we thank you that this child
has now been born again of water and the Holy Spirit, and has
become your own child by adoption and a member of your
church.' But we also go on to say, 'grant that he may grow in the
faith in which he has been baptised; grant that he himself may
profess it when he comes to be confirmed.' This indicates very
clearly that there is an onus on us to claim our inheritance of
baptism and to acknowledge and accept the fact of our regener-
ation, of our being born anew or from above, and actualise in
our own lives what is lying there dormant. The way Paul expressed it in his letter to the Romans (6:11) was: 'So you also

must consider yourselves dead to sin and alive to God in Christ
Jesus.' It is like a fire that can look dead, but is only waiting to be
fanned into life, and that fan is the Spirit which stirs to life that
wonderful litany of the fruit of the Spirit outlined in Galatians
including love, joy and peace.

The concept of new birth runs through the whole of the New
Testament. One of its best known expressions is in Paul's Second
Letter to the Corinthians (5:17): 'So if anyone is in Christ, there is
a new creation: everything old has passed away; see, everything
has become new!' And he links this closely with the idea of
reconciliation, that those who are born anew have above all else
entrusted to them the ministry of reconciliation: 'All this is from
God, who reconciled us to himself through Christ, and has given
us the ministry of reconciliation' (5:18). No matter how we interpret the words of the well-known text from John, one thing is
certain, we are not born anew in a vacuum. It cannot be a wholly
individualistic experience, rather it brings with it the obligation
to exercise a ministry of reconciliation as ambassadors for
Christ. Put at its simplest it means that by their fruits shall disciples of Christ be known. There must be evidence of an enriched
quality of life that reflects the fruit of the Spirit.

'Born from above', 'born anew', 'born again', are fine and
meaningful biblical phrases reflecting the breadth of meaning in
the original word. They are not the sole property of any one
group but relate back to the teaching of Jesus himself. They challenge us to a deeper personal commitment, a commitment
which will enrich our own lives and the lives of all those with
whom we come in contact.

CHAPTER 46

John Chapter 8, verse 58:
'Before Abraham was, I am.'

This is one of the central statements in the New Testament. It occurs at the conclusion of a debate or discussion which Our Lord had with the Jews concerning his person. Some of the comments he made had not only mystified but angered them. His opening assertion, 'I am the light of the world', was a challenge to their understanding of his mission. It was one of seven well-known descriptions that Jesus gave of himself, all beginning with the phrase 'I am', for example 'I am the bread of life' and 'I am the good shepherd.' Later on in the discussion Our Lord had even gone so far as saying that his hearers had as their father the devil because of their antagonistic attitude to him.

But now discussion had narrowed down to focus on Abraham, the father of the faithful, and venerated as few other Old Testament figures, the one to whom the divine promise had been made, 'In you all the families of the earth shall be blessed' (Gen 12:3). It is difficult to appreciate the position of dignity accorded to this ancient father figure. To be able to say 'we have Abraham for our father' was the highest claim a Jew could make, sufficient in his own mind to set him in an unshakeable position of privilege in relation to his neighbours.

Bearing all this in mind, we can begin to understand the reaction of the Jews when Our Lord said, 'Before Abraham was, I am.' They took up stones to cast at him. In their eyes the saying of Jesus was blasphemy, and according to the levitical law the penalty for this was stoning. Here we see Our Lord's breach with the Jews reaching a climax, and from this point on their hostility was to deepen until eventually it reached a final crescendo in the cry, 'Crucify him, Crucify him.'

But there was another dimension to this whole incident. If it had been simply a matter of removing Abraham from his exalted pedestal would this have elicited such violent reaction? Anger, perhaps, in much the same way as we might react to scorn being poured on one of our great historical figures, St Patrick or St Columba. However, to pick up the bricks lying around the temple and hurl them with murderous intent, as we have so often seen on our television screens, this was a different matter altogether.

And so we look for some deeper significance in Our Lord's statement, and we find it in the phrase 'I am'. Here we are led to the very threshold of our Lord's divinity, and it to this claim that the Jews react with such violence. When we read this phrase we immediately go back in thought to the Old Testament and to the Book of Exodus in particular. There Moses had tried to avoid the task of leading the Children of Israel out of Egypt. He had made a variety of excuses, that he was not a fluent speaker, that he was not an able leader. He even anticipated the question, 'who sent you?', to which the divine reply came back, 'I am has sent me to you' (Ex 3:14). This was the name which expressed the character of God as dependable and faithful. More than that, it expressed his eternity, and when used by Our Lord it was a sign that he was claiming an eternal dimension to his person. It has been interpreted by one writer as 'I am the eternal living one.'

It is this aspect of Our Lord's person that is referred to in the Nicene Creed:

We believe in one Lord, Jesus Christ ,
the only Son of God,
eternally begotten of the Father,
God from God, Light from Light,
true God from true God,
begotten, not made,
of one Being with the Father.

Or again in the Confession of St Patrick: 'Jesus Christ, who we affirm verily to have always existed with the Father before the creation of the world.'

This aspect of the person of Christ, his eternal being, is one that we must always bear in mind. Without it religion can easily degenerate into a type of secular social service, with a few moral principles thrown in for respectability. It is only as we retain an exalted vision of Our Lord as the eternally begotten Son of God, the great eternal 'I Am', that we are compelled to worship him. Rob Our Lord of this element, as we can so easily do, regard him simply as a moral teacher, and we rob our worship of all mystery, that element at the heart of true worship.

Some years ago a book was written with the very descriptive title, *Your God is Too Small.* It was an attempt to show how we can easily limit our vision of God, with the result that we are in no way challenged or filled with wonder by him. In more recent times controversy arose over the film, *The Last Temptation of Christ.* While certain scenes in the film caused offence to many people, the real and insidious danger lay in the over-emphasis on the humanity of Christ. Of course it is true that this must never be forgotten, he wept, he hungered, he displayed righteous indignation, he was tempted. Indeed without this human element we could not identify with him nor feel that he could identify with us. But an exclusive emphasis on his humanity gives a caricature of Christ. He is not only Son of Man but also Son of God, and it is this eternal dimension that gives us the hope of glory as we put our faith in him. He is the eternally begotten Son of the Father who existed before the foundation of the world. There is a need to rediscover this element in our faith. Not an easy task in our secularised society as we approach the end of the twentieth century. Yet we can aspire to it each time we meet for worship, because it is in worship that we are pointed beyond ourselves, and can begin to appreciate the significance of those simple but profound words, 'Before Abraham was, I am.'

CHAPTER 47

John Chapter 6 verse 35:
'I am the bread of life.'

The theme of bread is one which occurs many times in the bible. When the going got tough in the wilderness for the Children of Israel as they travelled from Egypt to the Promised Land, they grumbled about the lack of food. Initially so keen to come out of Egypt from under the harsh rule of Pharaoh, now they murmured against Moses and Aaron – 'If only we had died by the hand of the Lord in the land of Egypt, when we sat by the fleshpots and ate our fill of bread; for you have brought us out into this wilderness to kill this whole assembly with hunger' (Ex 16:3).

But having rescued his people, God would not let them perish and we read that the Lord said to Moses, 'I am going to rain bread from heaven for you.' And so God the provider sustained them with manna in the wilderness, with what literally was for them the bread of life.

In the sixth chapter of John we find Our Lord looking back to this incident with Moses and the Children of Israel in the desert. The chapter begins with the story of the feeding of the five thousand. Again it is the thought of God being a provider in time of need. But Jesus then leads his hearers deeper into the mystery of his own being. First he reminds them that it was not Moses who gave the bread in the wilderness. There is a constant danger that we elevate Old Testament characters beyond their station, forgetting that the real hero is always God, albeit God working through his agents. Our Lord then goes on to speak of the true bread from heaven, and makes what for his hearers must have sounded a most extravagant claim – 'I am the bread of life'. This was the first of seven 'I am' sayings recorded by John. Each says something about Jesus Christ and the role he plays in the scheme of salvation.

How then are we to interpret 'I am the bread of life?'

Bread is the great sustainer of life. It was so in the desert, and it was so for the five thousand. Here, using the same imagery, we are asked to think of Christ as the great sustainer, not in any purely physical sense, but in terms of eternal life. 'This is indeed the will of my Father, that all who see the Son and believe in him may have eternal life; and I will raise them up on the last day' (Jn 6:40). 'All who see the Son' – that is the real task of Christian living, to contemplate the Son and let his life story become a part of us, so that our minds become conformed to his mind. The challenge is to contemplate the Son in his totality, especially in his resurrection glory, which speaks of his triumph over sin and evil and death itself. This assures us that it is a living Christ we are called to contemplate, and not just a dead hero; not just a fitting example from the past; not just a victim of injustice; but a living Saviour who is the bread of life, the sustainer *par excellence*. It is not without significance that the symbol in many churches is an empty cross, reminding us of the victory of him who hung on the Cross and now is alive for evermore.

This thought of Christ as the bread of life is perpetuated each time we come to Holy Communion. 'Take, eat, this is my body' said Our Lord, and the bread which we break is a sharing in the body of Christ.

In the *Alternative Prayer Book* one of the themes on the first Sunday after Easter is 'The Bread of Life'. At first sight that might seem strange, but the more we meditate upon it the more we begin to see its relevance. The one who said 'I am the bread of life' is the one who rose from the dead, and through his living presence sustains us on our Christian pilgrimage.

CHAPTER 48

Acts Chapter 1 verse 8:
'You shall receive power
when the Holy Spirit has come upon you.'

Power is a commodity that comes in many wrappings – the horsepower of a car as it surges forward, the daunting power of the sea as it beats against the rocks, the emotive power of a speaker as he stirs the crowd.

However, for the Christian Whitsunday speaks of a particular brand of power – 'You shall receive power when the Holy Spirit has come upon you.' This was Our Lord's promise to his disciples immediately before his ascension. At that point they were probably at a low ebb at the prospect of losing their constant companion of the past three years. But with typical understanding Our Lord gave them a final assurance, an assurance of power, and this power was manifested in very dramatic circumstances on the *f*east of Pentecost as recorded in the Acts of the Apostles. There we read of the Holy Spirit entering into the lives of the apostles, transforming them from timid individuals into a band of confident witnesses. No longer where they cringing behind closed doors for mutual protection, rather like a ghetto in Nazi-dominated territory as portrayed in the film *Shindler's List,* but were prepared to go out into the world of their day bringing a message of joy and hope and reconciliation. They faced a hostile world fearlessly, and in the latter part of the New Testament we read this story. It's a really gripping adventure story as anyone reading the life of Paul in a modern version will realise.

But the dramatic events of the first Pentecost are long since past, and so we must ask, what of today? Is the Holy Spirit still active in the lives of individuals and in the life of the church? I believe we can answer 'yes' in both cases.

In the case of individuals, we see it illustrated in the call to holy orders. In our own diocese on St Columba's Day, three people will be made deacons. All in different ways have responded

to the prompting of the Holy Spirit to serve in the ministry of the
church. The first question put to them at the ordination service
will be, 'Do you believe in your heart that God has called you to
the office and work of a deacon in his church?' And that call is
made real for each individual by the Holy Spirit, God at work in
him or her. Of course this is not the only way the Holy Spirit
works in the lives of individuals, calling, transforming, guiding,
comforting, inspiring and strengthening. To borrow the words
of the well known hymn -

And every virtue we possess
And every victory won,
And every thought of holiness
Are his alone.

But what of the life of the church? Is the Holy Spirit still active in its midst? Again I believe this to be so, and at this time
each year we have it illustrated in the councils of the General
Synod, which was held last week in Cork (1994).

Throughout the Church of Ireland last Sunday, prayer was
made for those attending the general Synod: 'Mercifully grant
that thy Holy Spirit may rest upon them, enlighten and guide
them; and that all their consultations may be prospered to the
advancement of thy honour and glory, and the welfare of thy
church.' Those who attended the Synod will, I believe, be conscious
that the Holy Spirit was at work in their midst. I have spoken to
some who were there for the first time and they remarked on the
atmosphere prevailing. Not everyone necessarily agreed with
all that was said or even decided – not surprising given the
spread of people from every corner of the land. But people
spoke the truth in love even when they differed, and that surely
is a mark of the Spirit at work. Not just the content of our business but how we do our business speaks of the Spirit.

But the contents themselves also speak of the Spirit – concern
for those caught up in the cycle of violence in our own land and
elsewhere, particularly in Rwanda and the Sudan; concern for
the starving millions, particularly in Africa; concern for those
enmeshed in the drug culture of this Island, not least our young

people. These compassionate concerns spoke of the Holy Spirit at work in our deliberations, because the church, of all groups, must be a compassionate body and must be seen to be compassionate if it is to have any credibility in the eyes of the world. If I might quote again from one of our Whitsuntide hymns:

Spirit of mercy, truth and love,
O shed thine influence from above,
And still from age to age convey
The wonders of this sacred day.

Mercy, truth and love, these are the criteria of the Spirit in the life of the church. They were very evident in the deliberations of the General Synod last week, and I pray that they will continue to be evident in the life of our diocese when all the delegates have returned home.

CHAPTER 49

Acts Chapter 8 verse 1:
'That day a severe persecution began
against the church in Jerusalem.'

The church, using that phrase in its broadest possible context to include any individual who acknowledges Jesus Christ as Lord and Master, has been described in a variety of ways down through the centuries – the household of faith, the family of God, the Body of Christ, the fellowship of believers. Each description in a different way gives an insight into the nature of the church. As a household it is comprised of many members with different gifts and characteristics; as a family it is the context in which we learn to respect those various attributes; as a body it is living, growing, developing and changing, just as any vibrant organism must do; as a fellowship there is an intimate relationship between its members, nurtured especially by worship.

In the thematic approach of the *Alternative Prayer Book* we are also asked to consider the church as a community, and three distinguishing marks are set out – serving, witnessing and suffering.

It is not too difficult for most people to think of the church as a serving community. Service has always been at the heart of Christian commitment, and without it the church would be a very barren, lifeless and irrelevant institution. Nor is it difficult to think in terms of the witnessing community, which seeks to reflect the words of Our Lord, 'You will be my witnesses in Jerusalem, in all Judea and Samaria, and to the ends of the earth.' The difficulty is to apply these words in our modern complex society. But what of the church as the suffering community?

For most people suffering is thought of in individual terms, whether it be through sickness, mishap or misfortune. Yet just like service and witness, over the centuries suffering has been a part of the church's communal experience. This has been so right from the days when Christians were tossed to the lions up to more recent times in Communist countries, and on into the present day in countries as far apart as the Sudan and Myanmar. Why is it as we approach the third millennium that the followers of the Prince of Peace still suffer terribly?

If we look closely we will often find that suffering has to do with fear that embitters relationships – Arab and Jew, Hutu and Tutsi, Croat and Serb, Nationalist and Unionist. In so many parts of the world, it is not natural disasters that are causing suffering but fear. And the church, where it challenges the values of society, can end up being an object of fear, to be kept in its place. For example, in Salvador and Uganda archbishops, in being assassinated, paid the ultimate penalty of fear-filled reaction to criticism. Our Lord, by challenging the values of his day, became an object of fear, fear that people would run after him and follow him, and so he suffered the ultimate fate of death on the cross.

How is this fear to be countered? For the Christian it is only perfect love that can cast out fear. But love must have the soil in which it can flourish and grow, and that soil can be described in one word, equality. 'Love is possible only between equals' – such is the powerful phrase used by Gustavo Guitierrez, the South American priest from Peru, who has identified himself totally with the poor, becoming as one of them in their miserable situation in Lima, in order that he might preach the gospel to them realistically.

If love is the clue to the alleviation of fear, then people must begin to view their fellow men and women as equals. And they are equal in the eyes of God, that is the crucial point, not carbon copies, but all equally worthy of respect as children of God made in his image and likeness. Through all the dark years of apartheid in South Africa this was the message the church kept hammering home and eventually it won through.

And so as we contemplate the theme, the suffering community, we pray not just that we may be given grace to endure the sufferings of this present time, but that we may be enabled to banish that fear which is at the root of so much suffering, by recognising the worth of each individual in the eyes of God.

CHAPTER 50

Acts Chapter 11 verse 24:
'A good man, full of the Holy Spirit and of faith.'

These words describe one of the saints of the church. Not one of the more familiar saints such as Peter or John, but Barnabas, whose feast day is celebrated on 11 June.

Not too much is known about Barnabas. From Acts 4 we learn that originally he was called Joseph, that he was a Levite and therefore would have had certain duties to perform in the temple, and that he was a native of Cyprus. He was one of that early band who sold their worldly possessions in order to pool their resources for the good of all, and so engage in a type of Christian, non-political communism. In fact he sold a field and brought the money to the apostles, and in that way became identified with the new, and in a real sense revolutionary movement, Christianity, which was just beginning to gain momentum. It was when he came to the apostles that he was given the name Barnabas, which means 'Son of Consolation' or 'Son of Encouragement'. The appropriateness of these two titles is borne out by the life of Barnabas.

In the first place, he was willing to take a chance on Paul and accompany him on a hazardous missionary journey. Think for a moment about Paul. He had a past. He had been the great persecutor of the early church, and many a believer found himself in prison because of Paul's activity. But he had a life-changing experience on the Damascus Road, that dramatic about turn on his spiritual pilgrimage.

Yet despite this there were obviously some who still thought of him as the persecutor of the church, and found it difficult to accept him for what he now was, the great champion of the Christian faith. But not so Barnabas. He was prepared to join forces with Paul, and was happy to recognise the new role he had assumed.

It is so easy to dwell on the past and harp back to what has been. It is one of the scars on our national life, this ability to pay lip service to the future but give homage to the past. And this can so easily rub off on us as individuals, not least in our personal relationships. It was so even in biblical times. 'Is not this the carpenter' (Mk 6:3) was the rather superior comment once passed about Our Lord. But from Barnabas we learn to accept people as they are or have become. Saul the persecutor was now Paul the champion of the faith, and was accepted as such by Barnabas. How apt then was his name, 'Son of Encouragement', for what can be more encouraging than to be accepted for what we are?

This particular trait is further illustrated by another incident from the life of Barnabas. On one of the missionary journeys the young man, John Mark, had returned home. He may have found the going too tough. When a second journey was planned there was a difference of opinion as to whether he should be taken or not. Paul was dead against taking him, but Barnabas supported the young man and was keen to give him a second chance. So definite was he in this that he left Paul and took Mark under his wing. In doing so he may well have saved that young man from a feeling of inadequacy, even a life of despair. Again, how apt that title, Son of Consolation or Encouragement, was to prove for one prepared to give a fellow human being a second chance.

Today this attitude of despair looms large in a society haunted by the spectre of unemployment. 'It has hit like a hurricane,' is the way David Blakeley, a former Minister for Labour in the Northern Ireland Assembly, once put it at a General Synod in the early 1980s, when it was reckoned that there were thirty million unemployed in Europe. At that time the Church of Ireland urged society to explore the value of such concepts as job sharing and voluntary work. The Role of the Church committee suggested examining the controversial notion of a basic minimum wage for all citizens and families. The committee's words of fifteen years ago make interesting reading today: 'People would receive this minimum income, not because they have a job, but because they are members of a society who are rewarded financially by the community and encouraged to contribute to the welfare of society as a whole. Such a scheme would enable people to train, to develop and use their skills and talents in a wide variety of ways to the enrichment of the community. It would also preserve a sense of human dignity and value.'

This is our point of contact with Barnabas. He enabled John Mark to preserve a sense of human dignity and value. The church, of which he was one of the early pillars, must be no less positive in its approach in seeking ways whereby people can live in dignity. Not until we do this will we be worthy to be listed as the inheritors of the Son of Consolation and Encouragement.

CHAPTER 51

Romans Chapter 8 verse 6:
'To set the mind on the flesh is death,
but to set the mind on the Spirit is life and peace.'

The words 'flesh' and 'Spirit' form a recurring theme in Romans Chapter 8. In the total context of the bible they are familiar words, but as used by Paul they have a particular significance.

'Flesh' occurs many times in the bible with a variety of meanings.

(1) It is used, rather obviously, of that part of a human or animal which can be touched or handled. For example, the Israelites before leaving Egypt were instructed to eat the flesh of the passover lamb.

(2) Again, the word 'flesh' is used to denote near relationship, for example, a brother, while the term 'one flesh' is used of two people who are joined together in marriage.

(3) Sometimes the word is used of any earthly creature in contrast to God, emphasising human dependence on God – 'All flesh is grass, and all its beauty is like the flower of the field ... The grass withers, the flower fades; but the word of our God will stand for ever.' Human frailty is contrasted with the everlasting character of God.

However, in Romans Chapter 8 'flesh' takes on a more profound meaning. Here it is used by Paul to denote the seat of sin, or our human nature as tainted or contaminated by sin. By way of contrast, he speaks of the 'Spirit' as the divine or supernatural power which is at work in those who have committed their lives to Christ, God active and at work.

In a very real sense these verses contain the essence of the Christian faith. Paul points out that because Christ was offered as a sacrifice for sin, all those who are united with him are enabled to live and grow according to the Spirit, i.e. they are empowered to fight and overcome sin; they have the inner resources which are so necessary. And we are united with Christ as we are enfolded in his family at baptism, as we consciously commit our lives to him, and as we use the means of grace at our disposal, prayer, sacrament, worship and scripture.

But it might well be asked, is there really such a contrast between 'flesh' and 'Spirit'? Is it literally a matter of life and death as Paul would have us believe? Is it true that ' to set the mind on the flesh is death, but to set the mind on the Spirit is life and peace?' Paul himself draws out the contrast in clear terms in another of his letters, Galatians 5:19-31. There he lists the works of the flesh and the fruit of the Spirit. There is a familiar ring about the works of the flesh such as immorality, impurity, drunkenness, strife, jealousy and anger. Over against these is set the fruit of the Spirit: love, joy, peace, kindness, faithfulness, temperance. It has been said that it all turns on which of these two irreconcilable foes gains the upper hand in a person's life. There can be no compromise. Those who live on the level of the flesh have their whole outlook formed by it and their character determined by it. It may be the gratification of the senses or the acquisition of power, but the end result is the same, to be ensnared and caught up in a mood of selfishness. It leads to spiritual bankruptcy and the deadening of human sensitivity, which ultimately results in exclusion from the kingdom of God – 'Those who do such things shall not inherit the kingdom of God' (Gal. 5:21).

Today we live in a society where the works of the flesh are rampant. Immorality is commonplace with its attendant quota of human pain. Drunkenness is almost a way of life and recognised, even glorified, as a national characteristic. Strife and anger continue to result in tragedy. Yet the Christian can offer a more excellent way, the way of surrender to the Spirit which leads to life and peace. When this happens the direction of life is altered. The motives and priorities of life are dictated, not by selfishness which is the hallmark of the flesh, but by a concern for others. This in turn leads to the growth of a personality where love, joy, peace and the other fruits of the Spirit are the dominant characteristics.

As is so often the case with the words of scripture, they come winging their way over the centuries with a relevance that is startling. They speak to our contemporary situation in the most direct manner possible, reminding us that there can be no compromise with the flesh, that selfish, sin-laden instinct, which can so easily raise its ugly head.

However, the voice of scripture is not purely negative as is sometimes portrayed. It reminds us also that there is an alternative way of life which can bring true satisfaction and fulfilment, a more excellent way, because 'to set the mind on the flesh is death, but to set the mind on the Spirit is life and peace.'

CHAPTER 52

Romans Chapter 15 verse 28:
'So, when I have completed this,
and have delivered to them what has been collected,
I will set out by way of you to Spain.'

'I've been to the mountain top, and I've looked over, and I've seen the promised land. I may not get there with you...' Many people are familiar with these words from Martin Luther King's famous, indeed prophetic, speech given at Memphis on the day before his assassination in 1968. But dotted throughout his speeches and sermons are many quotable quotes, many powerful phrases, which sum up so much of what this great man believed in and for which he fought throughout his life.

One such phrase is 'Shattered dreams are the hallmark of our mortal life' and is contained in a sermon which has a very interesting text taken from the closing words of Paul's letter to the Romans, 'I will set out by way of you to Spain.'

These words might easily slip by unnoticed. Coming at the end of a letter which throbbed with theological life, and which by any standards is a learned treatise dwelling on the doctrinal and practical implications of the gospel, they might well appear as a conventional conclusion in much the same vein as saying 'The next time I'm passing I must drop in to see you,' or, 'When I'm passing through to Spain I'll call on you.'

For those who regularly take their holidays in Spain today it is probably hard to realise that there was a time when that area represented the extremity of the then known world. For Paul to speak of going to Spain would probably have entailed the same elements of risk and uncertainty as going to some uncharted areas of South America today. But Paul with his missionary zeal longed to spread the gospel and share with others something of the experience he had on the Damascus Road, something of that freedom from the bondage to sin which the law could not provide, and only came to him with the realisation that Christ died for sin on the Cross. His certainty and his enthusiasm, coupled with the support of the church in general, sent him on his three missionary journeys. But he longed to go further afield, beyond the centres of civilisation, beyond Ephesus, Athens and Corinth and the other cities he visited, to the outposts of habitation. Hence his dream of visiting Spain.

However his dream was to remain unfulfilled. Instead he found himself in prison in the very city of Rome to which his letter had been directed. Such was his shattered dream. But as Martin Luther King said, 'Shattered dreams are the hallmark of out mortal life.' And how true this is. We long to fulfil an ambition; we have high hopes in terms of work or travel or personal relationships; we set our sights on a particular goal, but something happens to alter the course of our lives and our dreams never become a reality.

In such circumstances, what is our reaction? It may take a variety of forms. We may rebel against a world which we believe has thwarted us. We may become cynical and hardened, with an attitude characterised by 'why should this happen to me?' Or we may withdraw into ourselves. In our disappointment we vest ourselves with a shell of isolation, often bemoaning the fact that no-one will relate to us when it is we ourselves who have caused the breach in relationships. Or again we may adopt a fatalistic attitude and talk of cruel fate, an attitude which ultimately leaves us devoid of any initiative. 'What is to be will be' we say, as though everything about our lives was determined by forces outside ourselves. A number of negative approaches which often accompany our shattered dreams.

Yet there is another approach, and it involves facing up to the situation and using it in a creative way. Paul highlights this possibility. Not for him was it a matter of languishing in a prison cell. Rather it was from his prison cell that he wrote some of his most memorable letters, just as many years later John Bunyan was to write *Pilgrims Progress* from Bedford gaol and Dietrich Bonhoeffer his *Letters and Papers from Prison* from Tegel prison in Berlin. What a legacy has been left to us from Paul's prison cell, and how much the Christian church owes to his jail journals.

But not only did he write in prison, it was there also that people came to visit him, and in that unlikely setting learnt something of the love of God revealed in Jesus Christ. As they went out from his prison cell his influence must have gone with them and been instrumental in building up the kingdom of God. In other words, Paul used the opportunity provided by his shattered dreams in a positive way. This is what he had urged the Ephesians to do when he wrote to them from Rome and said, 'Redeem the time', or to put it in the simpler language of some modern versions of the bible, 'make the most of the time or of every opportunity.'

It is given to few people, if any, to go through life without some shattered dreams, without some disappointments or hopes unfulfilled. What matters is how they react in these circumstances. They can, and indeed often do, react negatively as we have seen. But from the life of Paul we learn what can be accomplished by the grace of God when the response to shattered dreams is positive and creative.

CHAPTER 53

1 Corinthians Chapter 14 verse 15:
'I will sing praise with the spirit,
but I will sing praise with the mind also.'

To think of Handel and Bach, whose tercentenaries were celebrated in 1985, is to think of sacred music, and the life of all our
churches would be much the poorer without the contributions
they have made. The oratorios of Handel and the preludes and
fugues of Bach are an integral part of the musical traditions of all
churches. Indeed their contributions have been a unifying factor
in religious life. People from varied Christian traditions have
gained inspiration from listening to and performing their works.
Handel's *Messiah* and Bach's *B Minor Mass* are not confined
within denominational straitjackets, and we have good cause to
thank God for the lives of two men who, with distinctive styles,
have enriched the whole of life.

Although to think of sacred music is not necessarily to think
of hymns, for many people hymns are the point at which sacred
music touches the heart. It is the point at which they themselves
can become personally involved. 'Let who will preach the sermon,
but leave the hymns to me,' said Bishop F. R. Barry, a famous com-
municator of the faith in the earlier part of this century. In saying
that he was not in any sense downgrading the sermon, but
rather recognising the vital role played by hymns in the life of
the church, a fact reinforced by the popularity of the television
programme *Songs of Praise.*

Both Handel and Bach were products of an era, the first half
of the eighteenth century, which was characterised by a development of keyboard instruments. But of even more importance
from the church's point of view, it was an era when hymn writing began to gather momentum. Such famous hymn writers as
Isaac Watts, Charles Wesley and John Newton were producing
hymns of lasting value, hymns such as *When I survey the won-
drous cross* (Watts), *Love Divine all loves excelling* (Wesley), and
'Glorious things of thee are spoken (Newton).

Bach's great contribution to this movement was in the field of harmonisation. For example, some thirty-one melodies in the *Church of Ireland Hymnal* owe their harmonisation to his musical genius. On the other hand, just two hymn tunes in the same hymnal are associated with Handel. The first is *Rejoice the Lord is King,* that wonderful hymn of joy and hope written by Charles Wesley. It so attracted Handel that he composed the well-known tune *Gopsal,* which so perfectly matches the mood of the words. The second hymn is also a hymn of joy by Isaac Watts, *I sing the almighty power of God.* It is a great paen of praise to the Creator, and the tune, which once more enhances the words, has been adapted from the air *What though I trace* from Handel's oratorio *Solomon.*

However, in more recent times it is the music from the chorus *Lo the conquering hero comes* from Handel's *Judas Maccabaeus* which has caught the imagination. Christmas Eve for many people would be incomplete without the stirring rendering of *Hark the Herald Angels sing* from St Patrick's Cathedral, Dublin, where the familiar words of Charles Wesley are wedded to Handel's music with dramatic effect.

On a wider canvas, this same tune has virtually become the signature tune of the ecumenical movement, as it is allied to the words of *Thine be the glory, risen, conquering Son,* and sung in a variety of languages wherever Christians meet.

Many men and women, through their poetical and musical genius, have enriched the worshipping life of all our churches. Today we give thanks in particular for two such people, Johann Sebastian Bach and George Frederic Handel. God richly endowed them with gifts which they used to his glory. Bach in addition was a church organist and choirmaster for most of his life. Their sacred music is timeless and has enabled many to experience something of the mystery and majesty of God.

CHAPTER 54

1 Corinthians Chapter 3 verse 11:
'For no one can lay any foundation other than the one
that has been laid; that foundation is Jesus Christ.'

The concept of a good foundation is dear to the heart of Paul. It
was to the fore when he gave advice to the young church leader,
Timothy, and spoke of God's firm foundation (2 Tim 2:19), and
again when the Christians at Ephesus were commended for having the apostles and prophets as their spiritual foundation (Eph
2:20). But here in his first letter to the Corinthians Paul makes his
most memorable reference to a foundation when he says, 'For no
one can lay any foundation other than the one that has been laid;
that foundation is Jesus Christ.'

The context is interesting. He had already alluded to the dan-
gers of hero or personality worship. He spoke very strongly of
the jealously and strife among the Corinthians, a reminder that
we must be careful not to view the early church through rose
coloured spectacles. In this case one claimed to be a follower of
Paul, another of Apollos, another of Cephas, another of Christ, a
reminder that it is all too easy to exalt the messenger above the
message. So Paul goes on to ask, 'What then is Apollos? What is
Paul?' And he gives the answer, 'Servants through whom you
came to believe, as the Lord assigned to each.'

He then proceeds to spell this out more clearly, 'I planted,
Apollos watered, but God gave the growth.' 'Like a skilled master builder,' he says, 'I laid a foundation,' and he drives home
the unique nature of that foundation by adding, 'For no one can
lay any foundation other than the one that has been laid; that
foundation is Jesus Christ.' It is the thought expressed in one of
our best known hymns, *The Church's one foundation is Jesus Christ
her Lord.*

What then are the marks of this unique foundation?

Fundamentally it must be Christ-centred. Yet this is so often
the initial hurdle at which we fall down. We can test the Christ-

centredness of our faith by asking a simple question: 'What in the past year has dominated my religious thinking, and what issues have been at the forefront of my concern?' Upon our answer to that question will depend the nature of our church, our diocese, our parish, and their attraction to those who are on the fringe and seeking to deepen their faith and grow more mature in it.

If then our faith is Christ-centred, what are some of the characteristics it should display?

(1) In the first place, it must be personal. It is not enough to look back to the days of Patrick or Brigid or Kieran, and bask in their reflected glory, and live off the ecclesiastical crumbs that fall from the historical table. Our faith must be contemporary and personal.

(2) In the second place, it must be communal. It is in community that our faith is worked out as we seek to follow in the footsteps of him who fed the hungry, healed the sick and befriended the sinner. Down through the centuries the church at its most authentic has led the way in so many areas of communal work, medical, social and educational, and it is still so today.

Within the Irish context there is a particular challenge posed by the communal element in our faith. As a minority body we must not be lured into a ghetto-style existence. Over and over again in recent times public representatives have said to me that Irish society needs the voice of the Church of Ireland. It is the voice of reason and compassion; it is the voice that seeks to reflect the mind of Christ as it is revealed in holy scripture. Without that voice the Ireland of the twenty-first century will be a poorer and, dare one say it, a harsher place.

(3) In the third place, a Christ-centred faith must be consistent. Here is one of the great challenges facing Christians at all levels, how to live out a consistent faith in the midst of the complexities of modern society. There is, for example, the moral dilemma of the employee who disagrees with his or her employer's method of operation, and yet his own livelihood and that of his family is dependent on obeying orders. It is difficult to be consistent faith-

wise in the market-place, yet that is where faith must be lived out. One of the most recent examples is that of Desmond Tutu who, prior to the ending of apartheid in South Africa, lived a consistent Christian faith at a time when to do so endangered one's life. But he and others did not allow their faith to be determined by political and cultural considerations. In obeying God rather than men they were consistent.

(4) Fourthly, at the heart of a Christ-centred faith is the notion of forgiveness. As sinners we claim forgiveness because of what Christ has done for us on the Cross. He nailed our sins to the tree. But the demand made upon us is to reflect the forgiveness of God in our lives by extending forgiveness to our fellow men and women – 'Forgive us our trespasses as we forgive those who trespass against us'. We cannot really expect the mercy of God to be shown to us unless we are prepared to show forgiveness to others.

(5) A fifth characteristic is joy, joy issuing from thanksgiving for what God in Christ has done – the freedom he has opened up for those who have faith in him. It is not without significance that among those who express the greatest joy in their worship are the Afro-American people in the USA, many of whom only comparatively recently emerged from slavery. One of their freedom songs contains the very appropriate line, 'I sing because I'm happy, I sing because I'm free.'

(6) One final element that should be present in a Christ-centred faith is wonder or awe.

One of the sad features of modern society is a loss of wonder. We take so much for granted as we press our computer keys and turn our TV knobs. Yet our faith is something wonderful, that 'God was in Christ reconciling the world to himself'; that for two thousand years people the world over have been prepared to die rather than deny the reality of a baby born in a stable in an obscure outpost of the then mighty Roman empire. This idea of wonder in our faith is encapsulated in the words of one of our hymns:

O thou in all thy might so far,
In all thy love so near,
Beyond the range of sun and star,
And yet beside us here:

What heart can comprehend thy name,
Or searching find thee out,
Who art within, a quickening flame,
A presence round about?

In these words we have expressed in a simple yet profound way something of the wonder, the mystery, the miracle, indeed the paradox of our faith – that the great incomprehensible God is also a presence round about. If we lose our sense of wonder the result is disastrous because we then begin to make God in our own image, to suit our own taste. We end up with an *à la carte* God, far removed from the God revealed in Jesus Christ.

And here we come back to where we started – a Christ-centred faith. But the total Christ, who calls for our personal commitment, challenges us to communal action and seeks for consistency in our lives; the Christ whose followers must display forgiveness, joy and wonder. How true are the words of the Primus of Scotland, Richard Holloway, 'It is almost impossibly difficult to be a Christian.' Yet no one can lay any foundation other than the one that has been laid; that foundation is Jesus Christ.

CHAPTER 55

2 Corinthians Chapter 4 verse 6:
'For it is the God who said, "Let light shine out of darkness",
who has shone in our hearts to give the light of the knowledge
of the glory of God in the face of Jesus Christ.'

The bible contains many contrasts – sheep and goats, wheat and
tares, those on the right hand and those on the left. But no contrast is more regularly employed than that between light and
darkness. There are in fact about 250 references to light and 200
to darkness in the bible.

Here in 2 Corinthians Paul takes his readers back to the opening chapters of Genesis as though he was wishing to underline
the fundamental importance of light. 'Then God said, "Let there
be light", and there was light. And God saw that the light was
good; and God separated the light from the darkness.' From that
point on the contrast was to be between good and evil symbolised by light and darkness. For example, one of the most dramatic plagues to befall the Egyptians, second only to the killing of
the firstborn, was the plague of darkness, which had a paralys-
ing effect. Again, Mark tells us that as Our Lord hung on the
Cross the whole country was covered in darkness. Whatever
form it took, this darkness was deeply symbolic of the power of
evil.

But by way of contrast, Mark then goes on to tell of those
who, on the first morning of the week, came to the tomb when
the sun was risen. The resurrection was proof of the victory of
light over darkness, and what more appropriate time to discover
the empty tomb than when the sun was risen. It was as though
the whole world of nature was rejoicing in this great victory,
symbolised by the bright dawning of a new day. Jesus Christ,
the light of the world, had triumphed, and the significance of the
words in the First Letter of John became apparent, 'God is light
and in him is no darkness at all.'

What are some of the characteristics of light?

(1) Light attracts.

In Ireland, and especially in rural Ireland, stories are told of mysterious lights on the bogs and moors that draw people to their doom, just as thirsty travellers are lured on by a mirage in the desert. So it is that the light of the knowledge of the glory of God in the face of Jesus Christ attracts a variety of adherents. And because this disparate group of people from many traditions are drawn to the one light, so too they must inevitably be drawn closer to one another.

Some years ago in Union Seminary, New York, I had the privilege of sitting at the feet of one of the great ecumenical leaders of this century, D. T. Niles, the Methodist minister from Ceylon (Sri Lanka) who preached at the service marking the inauguration of the World Council of Churches in Amsterdam in 1948. One evening over an informal cup of tea (and we must never discount the cup of tea in ecumenism!) he propounded a theory of unity. 'If it were possible,' he said, 'I would lock all the church leaders in a room and not release them until they had come up with a formula for unity.' At the time I thought that this was a good way to approach the problem. Now I am not so sure. Surely it is not a matter of bargaining but of growth, and of growth into Jesus Christ – of being drawn, perhaps reluctantly in some cases, towards the Light of the World who is Jesus Christ. The challenge is to allow ourselves to be drawn to the light, and in being drawn to acknowledge that we will join and be joined by other pilgrims on the way.

(2) Light reveals.

Light shows up what is tarnished. So too Jesus Christ, the Light of the World, the goal of all our striving, shows up what is tarnished in life, shows up what Paul so aptly describes as 'the god of this age.' Indeed we might with justification speak of the gods of this age. So much is contrary to the mind of Christ as revealed in scripture, and the works of the flesh listed in Galatians are of more than academic historical interest – immorality, impurity, strife, anger, and the rest that go to make up that debasing catalogue.

But lest we become complacent and think purely in external terms, may we look into the heart of our own particular tradition and ask have we allowed allegiance to our own tradition to become an end in itself? Have we allowed our own tradition to usurp the place of Christ so that we no longer reach out to him who is the Light of the World? Are we in any sense repeating the sin of division evident even in the early church when those at Corinth claimed to belong to Paul or Apollos or Cephas or Christ? 'Is Christ divided?' asked Paul, and that is the revealing question continually facing all our traditions. Light does indeed reveal. It reveals not just the futility of the works of the flesh but also the sincerity of our ecumenical striving.

(3) Light strengthens.

The patient recuperating is advised to get as much sunshine as possible. Today much is made of the SAD Syndrome, which is basically a lack of natural light. In the world of nature plants flourish in the sunlight, they grow strong and mature.

Although nowhere is Christ, the Light of the World, referred to as Christ the Strengthener, there is no lack of reference to his strengthening power, expressed most succinctly by Paul in his Letter to the Philippians (4:13): 'I can do all things through him who strengthens me.' It is with that confidence that we continue our ecumenical pilgrimage 'looking to Jesus the pioneer and perfecter of our faith' (Heb 12:2).

Terry Waite, in his book *Taken on Trust,* paints a graphic picture of his 1763 days in captivity, and not least of the darkness. At one point in his seclusion he was heartened by a ray of light. Its symbolism spoke of strength and hope. The way he described it was, 'A ray of light enters the room through a minute space between the metal window cover and the wall. Gently it pierces the darkness. It shines with a steadfast intensity and gives me hope. Light is stronger than darkness. Hold on to the light. Let it strengthen you.'

What more appropriate thought could there be to cling to for those who follow the ecumenical path, sharing a common source of light – 'Light is stronger than darkness. Hold on to light. Let it strengthen you.'

CHAPTER 56

Ephesians Chapter 3 verse 8:
'The boundless riches of Christ.'

Here and there in the bible one encounters a striking phrase, one which warms the heart and challenges the mind. Such a phrase is this one from Ephesians, or as it is more memorably expressed in the Authorised Version, 'The unsearchable riches of Christ'.

The words 'unsearchable riches' stretch the imagination and challenge our understanding of the Christian faith. We find an echo of them in the words of the psalmist (Ps 145:3): 'Great is the Lord, and greatly to be praised; his greatness is unsearchable', or again in Paul's letter to the Romans (11:33): 'O the depth of the riches and wisdom and knowledge of God! How unsearchable are his judgements and how inscrutable his ways!'

In one sense, the unsearchable riches are Christ himself. He is the goal of all our striving, because in him dwells all the fulness of the Godhead. In so far as we experience him, be it through the sacraments or scripture or worship or stillness, we come to know something of his unsearchable riches, and are thereby strengthened for service.

But in the letter to the Ephesians particular attention is drawn to two characteristics.

The first is expressed in 3:6: 'The Gentiles have become fellow-heirs, members of the same body, and sharers in the promise in Christ Jesus through the gospel.' To appreciate the significance of this one must understand just how exclusive the old Jewish dispensation was. One of the first major problems facing the infant Christian church was how far certain Jewish practices, e.g. circumcision, should be obligatory on those entering the church. Old attitudes always die hard, perhaps hardest in religion.

But Christ is to be a light to lighten the Gentiles as well as the glory of Israel. There is a distinctive universality about Christianity which is one of its glories, one of its unsearchable riches.

Prince and pauper, young and old, black and white, male and female, all find fulfilment in Christ. This is a thought highlighted in a familiar passage from the Acts of the Apostles. There Peter, after his vivid visionary experience of a sheet let down from heaven with all kinds of animals in it, was prompted to say, 'Truly I perceive that God shows no partiality, but in every nation anyone who fears him and does what is right is acceptable to him' (Acts 10:34-35). This is the message God sent to the people of Israel telling the good news of peace through Jesus Christ, who is Lord of all. 'Behold, I bring you good news of a great joy which will come to all the people.' That Christ is Lord of all is the first mark of his unsearchable riches.

The second mark is expressed in some more words from Ephesians (3:12): 'in whom we have access to God in boldness and confidence through faith in him.' The two words 'boldness' and 'confidence' have a positive ring about them. Those who accept Christ in faith can approach him with confidence. Sometimes we find this confidence exhibited most obviously by those with the least share of this world's goods. 'I sing because I'm happy, I sing because I'm free', so runs the old negro spiritual. Yet very often the negro of that era was anything but free in human terms. But he did have boldness and confidence of spirit to approach God. In our well-to-do society we must be careful not to loose sight of the fact that it is in Christ and through faith in him that we approach God with boldness and confidence.

'The unsearchable riches of Christ' – it is indeed a phrase worth pondering over and teasing out its significance. It reminds us of the universal appeal of Jesus and his all-embracing love. It reminds us too of the boldness and confidence which can be ours in turning to God our Father through Jesus Christ our Lord.

CHAPTER 57

Philippians Chapter 2 verse 5:
'Let the same mind be in you that was in Christ Jesus.'

I'm an inveterate hoarder of cuttings and articles from news-papers and magazines. Very often they never see the light of day again, or if they do they have lost their real significance and acquired a faded dog-eared look. However, occasionally one does surface which, despite the passing years, has retained its relevance. Such was the case a little time ago while looking through a file headed 'St Patrick's Day'. There I came upon a profile of Patrick written by one of my illustrious predecessors as Bishop of Cork, who later became Primate of All Ireland, Archbishop George Simms. Like all good writing it had about it an air of timelessness. One particular paragraph struck me as being especially relevant, occurring as it does within the shadow of St Patrick's Day. It had to do with St Patrick's day being an inspirational day.

'We find inspiration on St Patrick's Day,' said Dr Simms, 'from his personal faith, his stand for truth and justice, and his loving concern for the people he had come to help and enlighten.'

There are three thoughts contained within that quotation which we do well to ponder over; three inspirational thoughts.

(1) First, Patrick's personal faith.

From what we can learn from his writings, his faith was simple and based above all on the bible, the Word of God. His confession and other writings are couched in biblical language and are a reminder of just how steeped he was in the handbook of the faith, and the motivation this must have provided for his work.

In some ways our faith is a personal matter, a personal commitment. But if it remains at that level it becomes introverted, selfish and judgmental – far removed from the faith symbolised by this great cathedral (St Mary's, Limerick) where love of neighbour stands alongside love of God.

155

Why hold a civic service? Why come to a House of God? Surely it must in some way be an indication that faith is seen as informing actions, not least in the context of public service.

Speaking recently on these matters, the Archbishop of Canterbury, Dr George Carey, had this to say: 'Morality is not only about personal behaviour. We should try to do good in the decisions we take collectively about the ordering of society. Morality is about justice, responsibility, compassion and generosity to others.' And he concluded, 'The basics of a good society include both personal and public morality. Politicians who seek to address this with due care and in the right way deserve our understanding and encouragement.'

(2) Patrick's personal faith, his deep-rooted biblical faith, did not remain at the purely personal level, but reached out and was bound up, as Archbishop Simms said, with his stand for truth and justice. And this is the second inspirational thought, his stand for truth and justice.

In his day there was a limited context as he confronted the ancient druidic forces with the truth of the gospel. In our day the contrast is no less stark but infinitely more complex as the values of our ancient faith come under attack from many quarters in an increasingly secularised society. Not least of the values under attack are truth and justice.

'What is truth?' asked Pilate almost 2000 years ago, and the answer is contained in the affirmation of our Lord, 'I am the way, the truth, and the life.' In other words, our understanding of truth is bound up with seeking to bring the mind of Christ to bear on every situation. Yes! Truth has to do with tribunals and fact-finding missions and enquiries, with getting at the facts of the matter. But in a Christian context and from a Christian perspective, it has also to do with bringing to bear on the world and society what are sometimes described as the kingdom values, values such as beauty, honesty and purity.

Viewed in this light, the scope for taking a stand for truth is widespread – beauty in relation to the environment and how we treat it; honesty in relation to the media and how the news is reported and interpreted; purity in relation to morality both individual and collective. The possibilities are endless because 'truth' cannot be compartmentalised. Nor is it an *à la carte* menu to be chosen according to our personal whims. Terry Waite, in the solitude of his captivity as a hostage, meditated on these matters and in his book, *Taken on Trust*, poses the very personal and pertinent question: 'I want to know what it means to live the truth.' That is a question we could all take to heart both as individuals and as members of a variety of corporate bodies, because in an honest searching for an answer we will enhance our contemporary society.

But according to the Archbishop, Patrick took a stand for both truth and justice. In one sense justice is a form of truth because it seeks to bring life itself into conformity with the mind of Christ, and is summed up by a biblical statement such as 'the labourer is worthy of his hire' – is worthy of a just wage.

Here we open up a panoramic scene because, as part of an affluent Western society, we must ask in the Christian context some searching questions about our relationships with the underdeveloped countries of the world, and the part we play in perpetuating a scenario whereby the rich get richer and the poor get poorer. The statistics do not make good reading. 75% of the world's goods consumed by 25% of the world's population: or, the Third World paying back considerably more in interest to financial institutions than the total aid given by governments and charity agencies. One does not need to be an economist to realise the devastating effect this must have on the economy of these countries as people work, not to supply their own needs, but to repay their debts to a society where the profit motive rules OK. Or the next time we enjoy a cup of coffee, may we spare a thought for the minimal wages paid to local coffee workers as compared to the retail price in the shops.   Justice is not just a political concept. It is that of course, as we are constantly being reminded on this island, but globally it is also bound up with economics, and because we are all part of the global village we have a responsibility – we are our brother's keeper.

His stand for truth and justice – that is the second inspirational thought associated with St Patrick, a thought that has far
reaching implications in contemporary society.

(3) The final thought is in a sense bound up with what we
have been considering – his loving concern for the people he had
come to help and enlighten.

This concern for people must surely be at the heart of all public service and civic responsibility. And thank God that is the
case in large measure here in Ireland. Those who serve the community deserve our support. This does not mean that we the
public remain uncritical. But it does mean that we be objective in
our criticism, recognising the basic altruistic role of our civic
representatives. Again, some words from the Archbishop of
Canterbury are relevant: 'It matters that our political leaders
strive to define what is right and good. It is wrong to mock their
efforts to do so. We must know what kind of society we strive to
be, and what values we encourage.'

If the events of ten years ago are anything to go by we could
well be facing into a summer and autumn of discontent as we
move towards another divorce referendum. It has never been
the practise of the Church of Ireland to tell people how to vote,
nor will it be on this occasion. But it is the duty of the Church of
Ireland, as of every other church, to ask people, whether they be
public representatives or private citizens, to consider what is
proposed in the dual context of the real world of today and the
mind of Christ. And that is not easy to do, nor is it open to sim-
plistic solutions. Dean Victor Griffin in his recent autobiography, *Mark of Protest,* puts it like this: 'The idea of authority in the
Christian church as a sort of oracle, dispensing infallible and sat-
isfactory answers to every doctrinal and moral problem, is a fic-
tion. We have to work hard, think hard, pray hard to find the answer. Even then we may be mistaken.'

But apart altogether from the decisions reached, the manner
in which they are reached will be a measure of our maturity as a
society – a society which embraces a variety of minorities, whose
record of social concern, national identity, public service, and

not least Christian commitment can withstand the closest scrutiny. To quote from Dean Griffin again: 'If we are to behave like civilised human beings we must be prepared to listen, to understand and never to be so cocksure of ourselves that we foolishly believe that we have nothing to learn from others.'

A civic service is a moving occasion, bringing together as it does many strands of public life. But it is also a challenging event, because it reminds us that that elusive spiritual ingredient, the mind of Christ, must be brought to bear on all our words and thoughts and deeds if we are to lay any claim to being a Christian society – a society worthy to be the inheritors of the tradition and faith of St Patrick.

CHAPTER 58

Colossians Chapter 1 verses 19 and 20:
'For in him all the fullness of God was pleased to dwell, and through him God was pleased to reconcile to himself all things, whether on earth or in heaven,
by making peace through the blood of his cross.'

In recent times there has emerged a renewed interest in God as creator, God whose injunction was 'Be fruitful and multiply, and fill the earth and subdue it' (Gen 1:28). A dangerous brief to give to mankind, and one which has been abused through ecological disasters in South American rain forests, nuclear fall-out in such places as India and Russia, and water pollution in our own country. So often we have subdued the earth without a due sense of responsibility, and without fulfilling the other element of the injunction, which is to fill the earth and replenish it.

That lack of responsibility has been bound up with mankind's fall from grace. It has been because of our greed and selfishness that the earth has suffered, or to express it in theological terms, human sin has extended to embrace and effect the world of nature. The words of the Psalmist (Ps 24:1), 'The earth is the Lord's and all that is in it', have been overlooked, and instead we have fallen into the trap referred to in Deuteronomy – 'My power and the might of my own hand have gained me this wealth' (8:17).

Western Christianity, and not least the Irish version of it, has tended to regard sin specifically in sexual terms. Yet sin is much more wide-ranging in its targets, and not even the good earth escapes.

But the good news of the gospel is that sin has been conquered through the death and resurrection of Jesus Christ. He has overcome evil, and those who have faith in him can reckon themselves to be dead to sin. For some this is viewed in very individualistic terms. Christ died for me – end of story. Of course it is vital that we recognise this wonderful assurance. It is at the heart of the gospel and leads to that peace of mind which passes all understanding. However, the words of Paul to the Colossians call us and challenge us to explore more fully what this gospel means in terms of creation. Speaking of Christ, Paul says, 'God was pleased to reconcile to himself all things, whether on earth or in heaven.'

It is sometimes said that there was a cosmic significance to Our Lord's offering of himself. Because all the fulness of God dwelt in him, therefore his victory had more than human relevance. That certainly seems to be so for Paul. Not only does he point to it here where he speaks of God reconciling to himself all things, whether things on earth or things in heaven, but also in his letter to the Romans (8:21) he says, 'The creation itself will be set free from its bondage to decay and will obtain the freedom of the glory of the children of God.'

This concept of the reconciling of creation to God is a difficult one for us to grasp in so far as creation, while active in terms of growth, cannot be said to exercise responsibility. One way in which we can make sense of the situation is to look at it through the eyes of redeemed humanity. No longer should we view the earth as something to be subdued by and for the selfishness of mankind, but rather as something to be respected as the Lord's. 'The earth is the Lord's' – that is the nub of the matter. We are but stewards of it. The thought is so beautifully expressed in John Arlott's lovely little harvest hymn, *God, whose farm is all creation*. What a delightful way to think of the earth, as God's farm. And every farmer knows that he must care for his farm if it is to yield the best results.

So too with creation. Here in truth we can be fellow workers with Christ, and so help to add reality to those words from Colossians which speak of reconciling all things to God, whether things on earth or things in heaven.

CHAPTER 59

1 Thessalonians Chapter 5 verse 6:
'So then, let us not fall asleep as others do, but let us keep awake'

Sleep is a necessary part of the cycle of life. From a good night's sleep we wake refreshed and better able to face whatever the day has in store for us. But too much sleep can be harmful. It can foster laziness and represent a misuse of time.

Paul introduces the idea of sleep in his First Letter to the Thessalonians when he says, 'So then, let us not fall asleep as others do, but let us keep awake.' This is not the first and only time that sleep is mentioned in the New Testament. The most obvious example is the disciples in the Garden of Gethsemane. There, as Our Lord agonised, they slept, oblivious to the momentous struggle taking place. Sleep had claimed its victims.

More often the idea of sleep is used in the context of the second coming of Our Lord. Waiting for the bridegroom the foolish virgins slept, and when the bridegroom came they were unprepared, their lamps untrimmed. They had preferred to sleep rather than use the time profitably. Again, this was the context of 1 Thessalonians, 'The day of the Lord will come like a thief in the night' (5:2).

When Paul wrote this letter people still expected the speedy second coming of Our Lord. The words to the disciples at the ascension still had an immediacy about them which coloured people's thinking – 'This Jesus, who has been taken up from you into heaven, will come in the same way as you saw him go into heaven' (Acts 1:11). But one of the fascinating studies of Paul's letters is to trace the gradual fading of this immediate expectation. However, it was never completely lost, and has been incorporated into the creeds as one of the corner stones of Christian belief – 'He will come again (in glory) to judge the living and the dead.'

From time to time there has been an undue emphasis on this particular element of Christianity, often at a time of calamity or strife or suffering, when people turn to those passages of scripture that talk of wars and rumours of wars. Again, some have become obsessed with the physical return of Our Lord and forecasting the actual date, despite Our Lord's warning that no one knows the day or the hour except the Father.

As time went by and the immediate expectation faded, it was inevitable that alertness would be dulled. But the season of Advent comes each year to wake us from our drowsiness and remind us of something that is at the heart of our faith, however difficult it may be for us to grasp and understand.

So then let us not sleep but let us keep awake, awake not just in terms of the ultimate coming of Christ, the culmination of history, but let us keep awake to respond to the continuous coming of Christ. Christ comes to us in many ways, especially in the lives of our fellowmen and women – the deprived, the homeless, the sick and the hungry. As we respond to them so we respond to Christ – 'Truly I tell you, just as you did it to one of the least of these who are members of my family, you did it to me' (Mt 25:40). It is this which grounds the coming of Christ in the here and now.

This is one of the elements of the gospel which has been rediscovered in the twentieth century, and perhaps by no one more than Michel Quoist whose *Prayers of Life* have meant so much to so many people. The closing lines of one of his prayers sum up much of what we have been thinking. The prayer has the intriguing title *That face, Lord, haunts me.* In it he paints a word picture of a young man's face moulded by so many evil influences in society, influences which have been created and perpetuated by not responding to the challenge of the continuous coming of Christ.

Lord, that face haunts me, it frightens me, it condemns me;
For, with everyone else, I have made it, or allowed it to be made!
And I realise, Lord, that this boy is my brother, and yours.

And so let us not sleep, but let us keep awake, awake not just as we hope to respond to the second or ultimate coming of Christ, but awake as we endeavour to respond to the continuous coming of Christ in the lives of our fellow humans.

CHAPTER 60

1 Timothy Chapter 4 verse 12:
'Let no one despise your youth, but set the believers an example in speech and conduct, in love, in faith, in purity.'

The ecumenical pilgrimage is ongoing. At times the pace quickens as people come together in such contexts as Taizé and Corrymeela. At other times those on the pilgrimage appear to grind to a halt and the necessary spirit of adventure is lacking. Where then is this spirit of adventure most likely to be manifested? Is it not among the young people of our various churches?

What are some of the characteristics of youth which could well give impetus to the ecumenical movement?

(1) The first characteristic of youth is openness. There is a refreshing honesty in the comments of youth, and a discontent with anything that hints of hypocrisy.

How vital it is in ecumenical affairs that Christians from various traditions should be mature enough to speak the truth in love to each other, not harbouring suspicions or searching for ulterior motives, or being negatively defensive. On more than one occasion Archbishop McAdoo, then joint-chairman of the first Anglican Roman Catholic International Commission (ARCIC), said that in the discussions leading up to the production of the final report of ARCIC 1 there was much free and frank exchange of views, but always this was done in the spirit of love and charity, and with an appreciation of what each person's religious tradition meant to them. The same openness characterised the Inter-Church talks at Ballymascanlon, where radically differing views were expressed and received with courtesy.

Until this openness is present at all levels, it is unlikely that the ecumenical pilgrimage will move far or fast. And so we look to the younger members of our churches, with their frankness and openness, to give us a lead as we seek to break down barriers, especially at the local level.

(2) A second characteristic of youth is enthusiasm. Given a

worthwhile goal, there is no limit to the enthusiasm and hard work which young people are prepared to contribute to a cause. In a real sense, the initial impetus to the ecumenical movement was given by students in the early years of this century. They went out with the cry on their lips, 'the evangelisation of the world in this generation'.

In the last few years it has been said by many people that the ecumenical movement has slowed down. This may well be a superficial comment, because there must always be a period of consolidation, and travelling the second mile is often much slower than the first. Part of the problem is that we live in an 'instant' age. Instant food is available, instant buildings are commonplace, we can even have an instant garden if we wish to impress our friends. Instant comment is demanded by the media. How easy it is to carry over this mentality into the solution of problems, problems which are long-standing and complex, such as those posed by the differences between churches. People then lose heart when the instant solution does not appear.

In the face of apathy and cynicism it is not always easy to maintain enthusiasm. But we must retain our zest because the cause is a worthy one and in harmony with the mind of Christ. What is the reading on the ecumenical barometer? That is a question we can all ask ourselves and try to be searchingly honest in our answering.

(3) A third characteristic of youth is a search for spirituality. There is a genuine search for a relevant spirituality on the part of many young people today.

Again, the ecumenical movement can learn from this, because there is an ever-present danger that we become so preoccupied with the structures of ecumenism that we lose sight of the underlying spirituality which is the inheritance of all our churches. This thought is well summed up in the prayer of one of the great pioneers of the modern ecumenical movement, Charles Henry Brent, the American Episcopal priest who later became Bishop of the Philippines. 'Most of us,' he once said, 'are in our hearts devotees of the cult of the incomplete – that is, sectarianism.' And he went on to pray, 'Lord Jesus, whose will it is to fold thy flock and to make us all one in thee ... enable each and all to find thee and in thee to find one another.' 'In thee to find one another' – within that phrase there lies a clue to a relevant spirituality, and to progress in the ecumenical movement. However differently we may express it, wherever we may place the emphasis, Christ is the goal of all our striving, because in him we live and move and have our being.

If then in our ecumenical relationships there is a lack of those features which characterise youth – openness, enthusiasm and spirituality – and if we are overly guarded, apathetic and concerned with structures, then we do well to ask what priority is given to Jesus Christ? Where he is merely on the periphery then it is unlikely that unity will have a high priority. But where he is enthroned in our churches then we have a firm foundation for ecumenical activity, because it is only 'in Christ' that we can hope to find one another at the deepest level.

CHAPTER 61

Hebrews Chapter 3 verses 1 and 2:
'Therefore, brothers and sisters,
holy partners in a heavenly calling,
consider that Jesus, the apostle and high priest of our confession
was faithful to the one who appointed him.'

Let me begin with a quotation. It is from the biography of Michael Ramsey, former Archbishop of Canterbury, and the biographer is quoting some of the Archbishop's own words: 'When you are ordained deacon you have arrived. But being a priest – that meant far more to me than being a bishop. Becoming a bishop is an incident in the life of a priest. I sometimes forget that it is the day of the year when I was made a bishop – I never fail to remember on the day of the year when I was made a priest.'

That quotation underlines the importance of this evening's ordination ceremony. The fact that we are ordaining one for the Auxiliary Ministry in no way diminishes the sense of priesthood. Indeed there are occasions when auxiliary priests have opportunities to serve in ways denied to those in the fulltime ministry. Again, it was Archbishop Ramsey who stressed this when, almost forty years ago, he wrote, 'I regard the contemporary development of a priesthood which combines a ministry of word and sacrament with employment in a secular profession not as a modern fad but as a recovery of something indubitably apostolic and primitive.' And he went on to say, 'What we call our 'auxiliaries' today belong most truly to the apostolic foundation, and we may learn from them of that inward meaning of priesthood which we share with them.'

And so we turn to the Letter to the Hebrews, and look again at the words of our text.

This particular letter is generally attributed to a Jewish Christian, and as being addressed to Jewish converts who were familiar with the Old Testament. It is important to keep this context in mind.

The first phrase to note is *heavenly calling*. The call to serve in the ministry is a heavenly calling. The call of the individual is tested by the church, and all who are ordained have undergone a rigorous testing of vocation before setting out on the course of study prescribed by the church. Before the laying on of hands the direct question will be put – 'Do you believe in your heart that God has called you to the office and work of a priest in his church?. And the response is 'I believe that God has called me.' The heavenly calling is affirmed.

The second phrase to note is *consider Jesus,* but consider him under two aspects, apostle and high priest.

Consider Jesus the apostle of our confession. An apostle is one who is sent out – a messenger of God. Jesus was sent from God. In the words of John 17:3, 'And this is eternal life, that they may know you, the only true God, and Jesus Christ whom you have sent.' He is the supreme apostle, the one from whom all other apostleship grows and derives its meaning. Those called by God go out as messengers of God bearing the authority of the one sent by God, Jesus Christ.

Because of this the message of the priest must reflect the message of the one who sent him. It must speak of good news, sin forgiven,purpose in life, plenteous grace, acceptance. And there is ample evidence that this is the positive message the world needs to hear and for which it is longing.

But is this the message proclaimed by the Church of Ireland today? For example, how does the content of our preaching measure up in this respect? Recently I was interviewed by a media representative, and the discussion came round to the use of the pulpit. It was suggested that more use could be made of the pulpit for getting across views and opinions. I tried to make the point that the task of the preacher was not to express his or her opinions, which were probably of no more value than the next person's. However imperfectly, the preacher is a messenger of God, and in so far as it is possible it must be a case of 'thus says the Lord'. By all means there can be a careful use of personal experience which can ground the message in reality, but mere opinions – no.

In the second place, the writer of Hebrews bids us consider Jesus the high priest of our confession.

I mentioned earlier the Jewish associations of the Epistle to the Hebrews, and because of these it is important to look back into the Old Testament in order to identify some of the high priestly characteristics seen there. The high priest delivered instruction, especially in the form of the torah or law. Then he came to be concerned mainly with offering sacrifice, while overall he would have been regarded primarily as a mediator between God and his people.

This is the picture of the high priest the readers of Hebrews would have had in their minds. But now they were being urged to consider Jesus 'the high priest of our confession', Jesus who was the fulfilment of the old order, who by his death on the Cross and in his person had abolished the high priestly office in one sense and the sacrifices that were so much an integral part of that office. Yet the title was retained and even emphasised in this letter.

What would those first readers of Hebrews with their Old Testament background have read into the title? Might they not have seen the original delivery of instruction, especially the law, as reflected in the teaching ministry of Our Lord? 'Rabbi, we know that you are a teacher who has come from God' (Jn 3:2) said Nicodemus. Might they not have seen in the crucifixion and in the institution of the Holy Communion the climax and fulfilment of the sacrificial system? And might they not have seen in Christ the 'one mediator between God and man', superseding the representative role of the Jewish high priest?

Translate these thoughts into today's world and see them in relation to the modern role of the priest.

Consider Jesus – Jesus the teacher. Teaching is one of the main functions of the priest. 'In your ministry will you expound the scriptures and teach that doctrine?' This is one of the questions that will be put by way of examination. Over and over again in church circles there is a call for clear biblical teaching. It is part of our priestly duty to provide it, and to neglect this aspect of our ministry is to do less than justice to our calling as priests.

Consider Jesus – Jesus in relation to the Eucharist. In the report of the Commission on Ministry, published in 1981, this aspect of the priest's work was underlined: 'The calling of the priest demands of him that he be ... the man of the Eucharist. While the liturgy belongs to all the people of God, yet in the eucharistic celebration the priest acts, not as the people's, but as Christ's representative; and not only in the name of a particular congregation, but of the whole Catholic Church from the beginning.'

To be Christ's representative, that is the awesome responsibility of the priest, and that is why in the charge he or she is reminded, 'if it should come about that the church, or any of its members, is hurt or hindered by reason of your neglect, you know the greatness of your fault and the judgement that will follow.'

Consider Jesus – Jesus as a representative figure. And in the light of that consider the priest as a representative figure, not self-appointed, but with a sense of personal calling tested by the people of God. It is because our priesthood is not a man-made ordinance, but has been derived from Christ, that we are bold to obey Our Lord's command, 'This do in remembrance of me', and be men and women of the Eucharist. It is because our priesthood has been derived from Christ that we can speak the words of absolution – 'If you forgive the sins of any, they are forgiven them' (Jn 20:23). Recently a clerical friend said that he had been in a church on holidays. After the general confession the priest conducting the service used the collect available when no priest is present. 'You know', he said, 'I felt cheated.'

In the context of the ordination service, we are asked to consider Jesus the apostle and high priest of our confession. In so doing the way of obedience is charted, a way along which many have travelled over the centuries, sustained by the grace of God.

CHAPTER 62

1 Peter Chapter 2 verse 9:
'God's own people.'

This evening, in this historic collegiate church of St Mary, we celebrate the climax of this fascinating Festival of the Arts here in Youghal. It coincides with another great festival, Summer Madness, in Gosford Forest Park, Armagh, where over 3,000 young people from all over Ireland are celebrating their faith with all the exuberance of youth.

In a sense we too are celebrating our faith, celebrating it not in an obviously theological way, but by acknowledging the gifts, talents and abilities that God has given us. And what a variety of talents are represented here in the church, talents which owe less to the technology of modern science than to time-honoured skills passed on from generation to generation, and perfected through patience and the persistence of craftsmen and women.

Such skills have a communal dimension, in that they form a common bond among all members of the community. This perhaps above all else we celebrate, the sense of community engendered by the occasion, and this ancient church so intimately associated with the town of Youghal is happy to host the festival. It is a particular joy to see such a representative congregation.

Community is a precious commodity, let us make no mistake about it. It is a tender plant that needs constant nourishment, the type of nourishment it is receiving this evening. Without that it is in danger of withering and dying.

If I might return to the North of Ireland again for a moment. There a phrase often used is 'the two communities'. In a sense that is a contradiction in terms. It speaks of division, and of people standing apart from each other, over against each other. It speaks of intolerance, which, in its most extreme form, seeks to justify persecution and violence, even murder. Real community recognises diversity within itself and the right of people, within the law, to live their lives according to their own traditions be they religious or cultural, Indeed it is this diversity that enriches community, for without it there is bland uniformity and monotony.

Within this island there is a rich tapestry of traditions which over the centuries have blended together to enrich the national life. This town and this church stand as visible memorials to this process, and the church, with its carefully documented artifacts, lends a unique historical perspective to the whole community. The atmosphere of this place was so well captured by David Woodworth in one of the last articles he wrote for the *Church of Ireland Gazette* before his untimely death on 11 June 1994. May I read part of what he wrote, as a tribute to a former priest of this United Diocese and as a reminder of the heritage which is ours as guardians of this place of worship:

> 'This was a place hallowed by Christian worship since at least the sixth century. It boasted Saxon and Danish traces within its stonework. Old when the Normans came, the church had witnessed to the rise of Fitzgerald and Boyle, had heard the march of Cromwell's troops, and had been at one time the seat of an attempted university, founded before the College of the Holy and Undivided Trinity, 'near Dublin'! The sailors of many nations had worshipped within its walls. Their vessels had docked in the safe harbour, unloading cargo and taking on provisions for the great adventure of crossing to the Western Indies, the new World, the Americas. Some of them failed soon in the attempt, and their bodies lie within the churchyard's bounds. Merchants, adventurers, soldiers, colonisers – the church echoes to their memories. It feels like some church once set on a foreign shore – and yet it is entirely indigenous to its place.'

Such were some of the last words written by a gifted journalist. They are an unsolicited tribute to a building which is an integral part of this local community.

It is right that the church, not using that term in any exclusive sense but rather as those who claim to be followers of Jesus Christ, should be a builder and supporter of community. In the

Old Testament we learn how God worked through the community that was the Children of Israel; not by any means a perfect community; a community that suffered hardship in Egypt and setback in the desert; a community that occasionally disobeyed the voice of God and found itself taken captive; a community whose leaders were not always paragons of virtue. Solomon and David would have found themselves quite at home in today's permissive society. Yet despite the uneven life of the community and its spiritual peaks and valleys, God worked through it, and it was within that community the Saviour of the world was born and worked out his mission.

In the New Testament we trace the development of the post-resurrection community, the New Israel, described by Peter (1 Pet 2:9) as 'a chosen race, a royal priesthood, a holy nation, God's own people.' It is as though the concept of community is dear to the heart of the Divine – 'God's own people.' Here surely we have both the joy and the challenge of community, of community such as we are considering here in this church tonight, something which has about it a dimension of the Divine. Otherwise why meet in this particular setting?

The joy of community is bound up with what has already been alluded to, the sharing of gifts, skills and talents. But even beyond the creative human gifts we see on display there is joy in sharing worship through which we pay homage to our common God. Whatever our specific tradition, through our shared worship we are 'God's own people', a community experiencing something of that deep joyful unity which we believe is at the heart of the Divine and for which Our Lord prayed shortly before his crucifixion.

But what of the challenge of community? Surely this evening it must revolve round our willingness to go out from here enriched by our experience, and determined to bring that experience to bear on the community in which we live.

If the past three days, and particularly our time together this evening, can be seen as an occasion of joy, but even more if it can be seen as a challenge to live out real and lasting community, then the Youghal Festival of Arts will have accomplished much.

CHAPTER 63

Revelation Chapter 19 verse 1:
'Hallelujah'

Christians are often described as Easter people in recognition that their faith is based on the resurrection, and at Easter joy is the great theme of the church's life. This is reflected in a variety of ways. White, with its overtones of joy, is the dominant liturgical colour. Flowers, which create a joyful ambience for worship, are present in profusion. The music used in humble parish church and majestic cathedral has a distinctive joyful ring about it, with the centre piece of some services being the *Hallelujah Chorus* from Handel's *Messiah.*

It is that word 'Hallelujah' which more than any other indicates joy and praise in our worship. 'Praise ye the Lord' is its literal meaning, and it is found in a number of psalms.

In the final book of the bible it represents the great cry taken up by the multitude of heaven in honour of Almighty God – 'Hallelujah! For the Lord our God the Almighty reigns. Let us rejoice and exult and give him the glory' (Rev 19:6-7).

And so the bible, which begins with the affirmation of God in the very first verse of Genesis – 'In the beginning God', concludes with a reaffirmation of his power and glory revealed, not merely in his creative activity, but in his gift of salvation resulting from his triumph over evil.

From early times the term 'Hallelujah' has been incorporated into the liturgy of the church, reminding worshippers of the distinctive element of Christianity – 'Christ is risen – the Lord is risen indeed, Alleluia'. In some parts of the world 'Hallelujah' is not used in services from Septuagesima to Holy Saturday, about sixty days. It is used again on the day before Easter, which as a result is called 'Alleluia Saturday'.

It is in our hymns that 'Hallelujah' is most often found, and of the nineteen Easter hymns in the *Irish Church Hymnal* thirteen incorporate the actual word. However, it is in the simplicity of a children's hymn that the meaning is most appropriately applied:

It is the joyful Easter-time,
Let all sing 'Hallelujah'
The merry bells ring out their chime,
They ring their Hallelujah.

The church is bright with flowers gay,
And all Christ's people praise and pray;
For Jesus rose on Easter Day
Sing joyful Hallelujah.

THEMATIC INDEX